A Work in Progress

A Work in Progress
The prospects and potential of the world's youth

Edited by **Michelle D. Gavin**

International Debate Education Association
New York*Amsterdam*Brussels

Published by:

International Debate Education Association

400 West 59th Street

New York, NY 10019

Library of Congress Cataloging-in-Publication Data

A work in progress : the prospects and potential of the world's youth / editor, Michelle D. Gavin.

p. cm.

ISBN 978-1-932716-44-3

1. Youth--Social conditions. 2. Youth--Social life and customs. 3. Youth development. I. Current history (New York, N.Y. : 1941)

HQ796.W637 2008

305.23509'051--dc22

2008019187

Design by Gustavo Stecher, Juan Pablo Tredicce and Andrés Vanegas | imagenHB.com

Printed in the USA

IDEBATE PRESS

Contents

Introduction

Man's own youth is the world's youth; at least he feels as if it were, and imagines that the earth's granite substance is something not yet hardened, and which he can mould into whatever shape he likes.

—Nathaniel Hawthorne, *The House of the Seven Gables*

Today young people comprise a greater share of the world's population than ever before; the United Nations estimates that there are approximately 1.2 billion people aged 15–24 around the world. This collection of essays, originally published as a series in *Current History*, starts from one basic premise: the only thing worse than ignoring this demographic is to mistake it for a monolithic group, ignoring the vastly varied nature of young people's situations. In the pages that follow, a diverse group of writers explores the preferences, aspirations, and frustrations of young people in specific geographic and thematic contexts, providing real insight into the complexities of the modern youth experience, as well as the transformational potential and the special vulnerabilities of youth. The authors approach their subjects from different angles, highlighting the profound differences that cultural, political, and economic factors can bring to bear on the circumstances of youth. In the end the idiosyncratic nature of the collection illuminates how many questions remain unanswered, and how much is left to explore.

Recurring Themes

Despite this volume's emphasis on the distinct challenges confronting young people in different geographic regions and socioeconomic circumstances, several themes recur frequently throughout the essays, highlighting the unifying threads in the complex fabric of youth experience. Definitional issues, of course, come into play regularly. "Youth" is meant to apply to people who have exited from childhood, but have yet to fully transition into the adult world. While the United Nations generally sticks to its definition of youth as 15- to 24-year-olds, essays on African and European youth reveal that the age range of "youth" can be far more flexible, and that definitions can depend on social judgments or simply individual self-assessments. Popular ideas about what is meant by youth also vary according to one's cultural context. While a great deal of literature romanticizes youth as time of passion, idealism, and reckless adventure—luxuries that responsible adults can ill-afford—in other narratives young people are deferential and approval seeking rather than headstrong, and in still others, they are far more likely to be desperate survivors than quixotic dreamers. In some contexts youth and youth successes are symbolic of an entire country's rise to global prominence, and elsewhere youth are often cast in the role of menacing, destabilizing elements, threatening the existing social order. Indeed, in some policy-making circles, the very mention of a large relative population of young people, or a "youth bulge," is understood as shorthand for a serious threat to peace and security.

Some of this variation has its roots in basic demographic trends. While the relative numbers of young people are shrinking in the aging populations of Europe and parts of East Asia, a tremendous surge of young people is swamping the populations of Africa, as well as countries like Yemen, Iraq, Afghanistan, and East Timor. When young people are scarce resources, they are less likely to be viewed as a social problem than when their numbers are vast, despite the fact that youth can provide and have, in the right circumstances, provided a tremendous boost to economic growth. Migration patterns also affect this picture; millions of young people in Asia, Latin America, and Africa are proving willing to travel far beyond their native countries to seek their futures, altering age distributions in some places with a high density of young immigrants and adding layers of complexity to social ideas about youth populations.

As youth manage the transition from childhood to adulthood, issues of identity become particularly important. Young people's sense of self and purpose is still a work in progress while they remain outside the structures that determine the shape and boundaries of adult lives, but youth are typically not the objects of nurturing social interventions designed to guide them toward their futures in the way that children are. Several of the essays in this collection explore the ways young people express generational consciousness, reflect cosmopolitan sensibilities derived from their exposure to globalization, and yet still incorporate strong elements of national identity in their endeavors. From the patchwork of cultural references woven together by young Indians to the aggressive nationalism of youthful Russians, it is clear that young people around the world devote significant time and energy to thinking about their place in their own society, and that finding ways to express their allegiance and belonging to that larger, established group is often just as important as introducing elements of modernity, change, and individuality to their adult identities.

Youth are clearly interested in finding paths to participation — in the job market and broader economy, and in civic affairs. The UN's Commission for Social Development has found that almost half of the world's young people are unemployed; although young people make up only one-quarter of the total working-age population, an imbalance that exposes one of the most obvious and consistent youth problems. Even for those with access to higher education, barriers to entry in the formal economy can be nearly insurmountable. Likewise, the obstacles youth face in being taken seriously as stakeholders and decision makers in their societies can be formidable. Most of the authors ask the same fundamental questions about what young people want from their societies and what they are prepared to contribute, but several also note that it can be difficult to find methods of social interaction that make it possible to realize youth intentions.

The explicitly political dimensions (or lack thereof) inherent in the diverse youth cultures profiled here are particularly effective in illustrating the surprising and often unintended consequences of youth-driven change. The essay on Chinese youth suggests a preoccupation with joining in the capitalist experience, while political participation is less important. But for young people in parts of Africa, finding paths to access political networks is intimately connected with economic participation. More than one essay flags the dangers associated with failed or derailed efforts at social participation, as alienated youths may turn to illicit, criminal networks (as in Central America's gang culture) or simply languish in situations of ever-worsening deprivation.

The relationship between youth and armed conflict comes up in several essays as well, and for good reason. Social scientists have long been aware of the correlation between large populations of young people and an increased frequency of conflict. But these essays tend to take youth's point of view. Since young people, and particularly young men, constitute the majority of the world's war fighters, youth are disproportionately sensitive to issues surrounding military mobilization, although they may be among the least equipped to cope with the consequences of armed conflict. Indeed, this is one area in which participation by young people may be both relatively easy (in terms of accessing opportunities to engage in combat) and nearly impossible (in terms of influencing political decisions about conflict). Recurring themes become interrelated when one learns how youth-dominated militias in Ivory Coast used text messaging technologies to become powerful players in that country's civil unrest, while young Russians used popular culture outlets like film to express their views on the conflict in Chechnya.

Indeed, popular culture and technology are two powerful forces that appear with some frequency in this collection. Young people are influenced by images of material success that are often generated in the West's youth-obsessed pop culture and reinforced by sophisticated marketing strategies that target young consumers with precision, setting expectations that may be particularly difficult to meet in resource-poor settings. But youth also generate much of the content of popular culture, using a range of media to express those emerging identities and sometimes to criticize existing social mores or popular policies. Either way, it is clear that music, movies, and other cultural products are far more than diversions for carefree young people around the world—they can be profoundly important mechanisms driving social change. Relatively new communications technologies only reinforce this point. Young people around the world are adapting quickly to new technologies and using them to invent new economic opportunities, form new social networks, and create new spaces for their voices to be heard.

Despite the unifying themes that recur in this collection of essays, youth dynamics may reveal as much about the deepening gulf between the industrialized and the developing world as they do about the globalized nature of modern society. For all their cosmopolitanism, the young Europeans enjoying an extended period of self-discovery and the young migrants who flock to Europe in search of opportunity experience youth very differently, and it is not difficult to understand why tensions between these communities would be on the rise. As migration becomes an increasingly important part of the youth experience, mutual understanding may be far harder to come by than shared enthusiasms for technological advances or cultural products.

Responding to Youth

Several authors make reference to the way that governments attempt to harness youth potential or to tamp down young people's explosive frustration, and it appears that the range of official responses is nearly as vast as the range of youth experiences. Some governments seem nearly oblivious to their youthful populations, while others eagerly court the youth vote and seek to co-opt young people through numerous state-sponsored organizations and activities designed to integrate, and perhaps in some cases to control and to manipulate, the youth agenda. In still other cases, an antagonistic relationship between young people and the state develops as unruly youths become targets of aggressive and violent law-and-order campaigns, raising serious questions about the prospects for tapping the human capital of these youth populations or finding meaningful paths to civic participation in the future.

Some discussions in development circles react to the serious problems facing young people with a renewed focus on children's issues, essentially arguing that the most important priority is to ensure that the next generation of youth is healthier and better educated than youth are today. Indeed, in the foreword to the 2005 version of the *World Youth Report*, UN Under-Secretary General José Antonio Ocampo pointed to a number of serious structural difficulties confronting young people on the path to adulthood but concluded that "investing in youth starts with investing in children. Strengthening policy and resource commitments now with the aim of achieving the relevant MDG [Millennium Development Goals] targets in the coming decade will produce enormous benefits for the young people of 2015." Ocampo was right, but even strong, educated young people emerging from childhood cannot successfully enter productive adulthood if there are no bridging mechanisms to help them move from one phase to another. Some of the essays in this collection express support for such mechanisms, like job-creation efforts and policies designed to promote entrepreneurship. The UN's World Programme of Action for Youth highlights others, including the need for increased vocational training and civic education. But it is clear that much remains to be done to determine how best to help young people overcome the challenges before them and realize their potential. A close examination of the specific circumstances of youth around the world is a good place to start.

The Essays

Yunxiang Yan's lively piece, "Little Emperors or Frail Pragmatists? China's '80ers Generation," paints a vivid portrait of young people disinterested in ideology but energized and driven by material ambitions. The specific circumstances of his subjects—they have very few or no siblings due to population control policies and are too young to have any real experience of Maoist socialism—have driven them to develop their own extraordinarily goal-oriented pragmatic culture. And while this generation enjoys unprecedented individual freedoms and material comforts, these appear to offer little respite from intense intra-generational competition. The author's observations of the '80ers' relationship to their government are particularly interesting. These driven, achievement-oriented young people do seek party membership, but their enthusiasm is instrumental rather than ideological: party membership is perceived to be a valuable networking opportunity that could be useful in securing a lucrative job—and not necessarily one in government. In the end, Yan seems disappointed that this generation's energy and focus are unlikely to be politically transformative, writing that "if the seeds of social changes are to be found in youth, then the current generation of Chinese youth is the least hopeful."

Meanwhile, the young people of "India's Remix Generation" are also embracing modernity and consumerism in a competitive society. Rashmi Bansal writes evocatively about the magpie-like nature of Indian youths who pluck elements of old and new, local tradition and global trends, to create an entirely fresh youth culture that is creative and, in many ways, liberating. Bansal describes youth leading the way as their parents and other older Indians adapt to youth-driven change, and she illustrates how central technology is to this generation, enabling young Indian women, in particular, to explore new forms of social networking that give them more autonomy than ever before. Though the article acknowledges the vast disparity in living standards and lifestyles to be found among any age range of India's population, it also makes a compelling argument that the opportunities for socioeconomic advance are greater than ever before. In the end, meritocratic striving and technological advances have ensured that even in light of the dizzying diversity of Indian society, "in terms of culture. . . the youth of today are more unified and connected than ever before."

Russian youth are the subject of Thomas J. Garza's article, "Conservative Vanguard? The Politics of New Russia's Youth." His analysis traces the development of Russian youth culture from a directionless era of ennui in the late 1980s through the emergence of new social and cultural cliques in the 1990s to today's milieu of overtly political youth organizations. This essay tackles weighty issues, including the profound effect that military conscription and the Chechen war have had on youth consciousness and the emergence of zealously pro-government "youth movements" that are essentially sponsored, overtly or covertly, by political elites. But at the same time, Garza brings his subject to life with specific references to music, television, and film that reflect and inform Russian youth movements, clearly illustrating the power of popular culture in youth circles. It seems that the efforts of many Russian youth to forge a new, often explicitly nationalistic sense of identity—and the efforts of other young people to challenge this vision—find expression or validation both at the ballot box and through the arts.

Jeffrey Jensen Arnett explores "The Long and Leisurely Route: Coming of Age in Europe Today" in his insightful contribution. Addressing the fundamental issue of just what is encompassed by the idea of "youth," he explains the rise of a new phase of "emerging adulthood" that captures the circumstances of European youths from their late teens to late 20s. This time of exploration and seemingly endless possibility is driven by lofty expectations surrounding personal and professional life. Young Europeans are looking for lifelong soul mates and rewarding, meaningful work—and they are willing to devote years to trial and error in pursuit of these goals. Arnett recognizes the downsides, which include instability and periods of unemployment, of devoting so many years to this process of searching and self-discovery. He notes that immigrants unable to fully experience this phase of indulgent exploration may feel a heightened sense of alienation from their age-mates, and also acknowledges that the pace of emerging adulthood does little to encourage a higher birthrate, contributing to Europe's aging population and the strain this places on European welfare systems. But overall, the author finds the embrace of "emerging adulthood" among Europeans to be quite an admirable development, describing the consequences as "beautiful problems."

Whereas Arnett's European youths have individualistic ideas about what defines adulthood and are choosing to postpone assuming adult responsibilities, many of the young people discussed in "Africa's Restless Youth" are eagerly seeking an adulthood characterized by socially evident signifiers like marriage, having children, and stable employment. However, vast numbers of them are frustrated in their efforts to reach that adulthood, and are left lingering in the youth category long after they wish to move on. Born into an enormously large group of young people in states with often fragile economies, these young Africans are desperate for opportunities to assert themselves. They harbor a natural desire to affect social change that might provide for more promising futures, and this desire can find a wide range of expressions, both political and religious, both peaceful and violent. The article suggests that their power to reshape their societies—either as instruments of older elites or as autonomous actors—deserves far more careful attention than it has received to date.

Several authors explore the idea of youth at risk and the intersection between youth and violence. Richard Curtain writes about young people in low-income regions in his piece, "For Poor Countries' Youth, Dashed Hopes Signal Danger Ahead." He finds that improvements in education and health care, combined with urbanization and increased exposure to "the images and values of globalization," lead to heightened expectations among the developing world's youths. But with few opportunities available to them, these youths often come to be seen by others as vulnerable or destabilizing elements of society. Only rarely is the potential of youth recognized and understood to be an asset for developing countries to tap. Curtain underscores the critically important issue of job creation, writing that "the urgent question facing the developing world is how to improve young people's job prospects now." The article points to a number of answers, including policies and programs to promote entrepreneurship, improve access to microcredit, invest in labor-intensive infrastructure projects, encourage orderly labor migration, and build capacity through national service.

Cheryl Benard's thought-provoking "Toy Soldiers: The Youth Factor in the War on Terror" highlights recent scientific research indicating that the neurological development of young men in their late teens and early 20s is typically incomplete, rendering them more likely to make impulsive and risky decisions without adequate consideration of the likely consequences. Benard points out that this makes young men ideal targets for manipulation by elites, tackling head-on the special resonance that military campaigns, be they organized by states or non-state actors, have for the young. Young people wage these campaigns, assuming the greatest personal risk and making the most significant personal sacrifices, yet they are rarely among the campaigns' architects. Benard argues that many of today's violent conflicts are characterized by "an unspoken, disturbing social contract in which older people pursue agendas by deploying the volatile weapon of mentally not-yet-mature younger men." The consequences for these youths are as serious as they are for society at large, as young soldiers are more likely to experience post-traumatic stress disorder than their older counterparts.

In "Youth, Violence, and Democracy," Paulo Sérgio Pinheiro focuses on the plight of Central American youth. Pinheiro, who was appointed by the United Nations secretary general to conduct a study of violence against children, explains the complex pathology of youth and crime in which young people are both victims and perpetrators of violence, growing up in a toxic environment of brutality. As societies channel the fear and anger provoked by encounters with criminality into support for draconian "get tough" policies, the violence becomes all the more ubiquitous. Pinheiro urges more serious efforts to understand the circumstances of the unmoored, marginalized young people at the heart of this cycle, and calls for preventative policies to address the socioeconomic factors that provide a seemingly endless supply of fresh recruits for the *maras* (gangs). Particularly in the Central American context of dysfunctional juvenile justice systems and human rights protections that are far stronger in theory than in practice, the dangers of alienating young people from the law and the state threaten the integrity of democracy in the region.

For Further Exploration

Taken as a whole, these essays make plain the difficulties of generalizing about youth, given the tremendous diversity of circumstances and challenges that confront young people around the world. But they also suggest that youth issues are a great deal more politically and culturally important than is often understood. The articles raise as many questions as they answer, and underscore the urgency of further inquiry. Which job-creation strategies are most effective? How do young people socialized into violence become effectively and meaningfully integrated into law-governed, democratic societies? How can analysts obtain adequate information about the frustrations and aspirations of young people around the world when so many of these youths are alienated from the modes of civic participation that could give them voice? How can societies more effectively tap the capacities and contributions of young women in regions where their special vulnerabilities too often lead to their virtual disappearance from civic consciousness? Readers will undoubtedly develop questions of their own, and the potential for further exploration is as full of promise as young people themselves.

Going forward, it is vitally important to recognize that the nature of youth movements and youth consciousness is constantly evolving. Youth priorities and strategies change rapidly as new avenues for participation are discovered and older ones crumble. University student movements that could shake political establishments to their foundations decades ago may be utterly powerless today—and student politics may even be irrelevant in the eyes of the current generation, who may invest more time, energy, and hope in virtual networks that are global in scope. Cultural outlets that once figured prominently in young people's self-expression may become passé, and jobs or status symbols that were once objects of longing may be replaced with entirely new aspirations. Because change is a constant, regular, close examination of what is happening among youth populations today is critical to efforts to engage young people and ensure that they have a chance to play a meaningful and constructive role, not just a hypothetical or chaotic one, in reshaping our world.

"If idealism, compassion, and naïveté are defining features of youthhood, the '80ers in China are hardly youthful. If efforts to resist and subvert the dominating ideology and symbolisms of the establishment are the core of youth culture, then China's youth hardly have a culture of their own."

Little Emperors or Frail Pragmatists? China's '80ers Generation

Yunxiang Yan

In September 2003, the fast food giant McDonald's launched a commercial campaign featuring a new message: "I'm lovin' it." This commercial helped change McDonald's old image of selling cheap fast food to create instead a youthful, fashionable, even cool flavor. It spurred a surprising boost in sales. What is less known to the public but perhaps more surprising is that the creative ideas for this global advertisement came from several young Chinese who worked for the McDonald's marketing division in China. According to Larry Light, the global chief marketing officer of McDonald's, the Chinese team took part in a competition for pitches from ad firms around the world. It came out on top with half a dozen ideas and was voted the most imaginative of the McDonald's global network. "China just blew our minds. We didn't expect that kind of expression and joy," said Light. "Our expectation was for much more conservatism, much less individuality, and more caution."

In its Chinese form, the slogan *wo jiu xihuan* (I'm lovin' it) conveys a much stronger, imposing, and disaffected tone and thus sends out more effectively a me-centered message: I am simply loving it; who cares what you think! Such a message, with the image of a hugely successful Taiwanese pop singer sitting on the hood of a red Jeep, acutely resonates with the life aspirations of the current generation of Chinese youth who are determined to achieve instant individual gratification in terms of a pleasurable and comfortable material life.

Who are these Chinese youth? Do they think and act in the same ways as the so-called Generation Y in American society (that is, those born between 1980 and 1995)? Chinese youth, like their counterparts in the United States, are indeed individualistic fun-seekers who want to go beyond old social norms and create their own brave new world of cool. But they do so only in the sphere of private life and mainly through personal consumption. When they step into the public sphere to face serious social issues such as injustice, inequality, corruption, and entrenched political authority, they become rational pragmatists who carefully plan their moves toward well-defined goals, skillfully handle complex interpersonal relations, and demonstrate an early-maturing distaste for idealism. Given the social-cultural environment in which they are growing up, these young pragmatists are also fragile in both physical and psychological terms, adding another layer of complexity to their collective character. It is this frail pragmatism that distinguishes the current generation of Chinese youth from many of their counterparts elsewhere in the world.

Rebels Without a Cause

Using a broader notion of youth that includes both adolescents and young adults, China's youth amounted to 560 million in 2005, with more than 200 million of them between the ages of 15 and 24. In the Chinese media, these youth have been referred to as the post-1980 generation or "the '80ers," although some were born in the early 1990s. This is China's most dynamic demographic group; each year more than 20 million children enter adolescence.

The '80ers represent the first generation of Chinese youth who have no life experience of Maoist socialism, who in childhood have heard adults saying that "to be rich is glorious" and talking about "jumping into the sea (of business)," who were showered by increasing supplies of commodities as they grew up, who witnessed the ups and downs of their parents' pursuit of wealth, and, since their first day of schooling, who also experienced unprecedented pressure to score high on various exams. They also constitute the first generation of youth who are either singletons in cities or have fewer siblings in the countryside, thanks to the strictly enforced policy of population control in the 1980s. While receiving more parental attention, love, and investments (hence their nickname, "little emperors"), they also are expected to realize the unfulfilled dreams of their parents and make it big in an incredibly competitive society.

Individualistic, free-spirited, materialistic, competitive, rebellious, Westernized, modern—these are among the adjectives the Western media have used most frequently to describe and define the new generation of Chinese youth. They grew up drinking Coke and eating hamburgers, quickly developing a taste for hip-hop and watching NBA games. Defying parental advice, they dye their hair, pierce their ears, and wear trendy clothes in a restless pursuit of being cool. The ’80ers are well informed, too: a quarter of them have learned a foreign language (mostly English), more than 40 percent have had 14 or more years of education, and they make up about 40 percent of China’s 100 million Internet users. We also know that the current generation of youth, urban and rural alike, has grown up without much influence from communist ideology. This generation is open to new ideas, uninterested in party politics, and yearns for freedom and individuality. On these grounds, it is plausible to say the ’80ers in China share much in common with Generation Y in America.

Like Generation Y, for example, they are sexually active. The ’80ers have continued the sexual revolution that began in China among the 1970s generation. They have moved back their dating experience to secondary school (some even earlier), have been widely exposed to pornography and Internet dating, and have begun to separate sex in dating from a commitment to marriage—hence the emergence of recreational dating. According to a recent survey among urban Chinese youth, only 25 percent thought that premarital sex was improper, and more than 30 percent considered Internet romance cool. A 2005 investigative report by a northeast Chinese newspaper found that 22 of 50 high school students interviewed had had sex, while 42 of the group had dating experiences. Those who have not had sexual encounters by the last year in high school are called “pandas,” referring to their underdeveloped sexual desires. And the sexual revolution is by no means confined to urban youth. A 2001 marriage counseling survey in Guangdong province showed that more than 80 percent of young people in rural areas had engaged in premarital sex, roughly the same as for urbanites.

The rebelliousness extends beyond sex. Indeed, China seems to have produced its own antiestablishment punks—or "The New Radicals," as the title of a special report in *Asian Times* called them. Han Han, a high school dropout who at the age of 17 published a best-selling novel depicting the dark side of China's exam-oriented education system, is considered the most important representative of this group of new radicals. The fact that Han sold more than 2 million copies of his books and could afford to own five cars has made him the ultimate symbol of instant individual gratification not only for Chinese youth but for the general public. So much so that the Chinese media often praise as "individualistic" and "creative" his often exaggeratedly defiant and arrogant behavior. Han's not-so-unique proclamation that "it is my choice to do whatever I want and go wherever I want" has been widely quoted as the '80ers' motto.

This all-too-familiar emphasis on freedom of individual choice and expression among Chinese youth bears, however, an interesting cultural twist. Taking a closer look at Chun Shu, another high-school-dropout-turned-young-writer and the cover girl for the February 2004 issue of *Asian Times*, journalist Hannah Beech noticed: "Chun writes bluntly about her own life, but she stays away from the grander ideologies such as democracy, freedom, and equality that have often motivated her alternative brethren in the West." In an exchange with Beech, Chun explained her choice clearly: "Our concept of freedom is different from the West's. We want the physical freedom to travel where we want, work where we want, have the friends we want. But right now we can't be so concerned with spiritual freedom."

Here emerges an important feature of the '80ers in China. They seem to know clearly to what extent they can exercise their youthful agency seeking freedom and individuality and then they plan their activities accordingly. In general, it appears safe for youth to experiment and indulge themselves with anything that falls within the sphere of private life, but either as individuals or in groups they explore few areas in the public sphere. A noticeable exception is the rapid growth of popular nationalism, in which college students in particular and urban youth in general have played a key role. It must be noted, however, that almost all anti-Japanese or anti-American demonstrations since the early 1990s have been organized by student groups officially affiliated with university administrations (which means they are government-sponsored), thereby proving little about youthful willingness to cross boundaries into the public sphere.

Noticing this difference between private and public activities, Beech has described the radical Chinese youth as "dogs wearing electric collars that know just how far they can stray without getting shocked. No one's jumping the invisible fence, because if they do, they might just end up in a gulag." This insightful observation draws our attention to the self-censorship among Chinese youth. But it also calls for more questions because it, like many other such inferences, finds too direct a link between a social phenomenon in China (such as the indifference and apathy among youth) and the conceived red terror of communism (such as the threat of gulag).

In reality, the Communist Party has also undergone a transformation during the 25 years of market reforms and it can no longer control everything that happens in Chinese society. The risk of being sent to a gulag has been reduced to a great extent as long as one does not openly challenge one-party rule—which is probably not what Han Han, Chun Shu, and other youth would have in mind even if they were allowed to exercise their individuality in the public sphere. It remains questionable, therefore, whether Chinese youth are afraid of political repression when they keep to a comfort zone of material pleasures in private life. More likely, they are practicing a kind of pragmatism that usually belongs to more experienced and somewhat cynical older people.

The Careful Realists

Unlike their carefree and sometimes drifting counterparts in the United States, most Chinese teenagers and young adults are clearheaded about what they must do for a good life: earn high scores on exams, gain admission to a prestigious university, and secure a high-income job. China scholar Stanley Rosen calls this the victory of materialism and pragmatism. After combing through rich survey data, he concluded that Chinese youth "have become less reluctant to acknowledge openly that instrumental, success-oriented values take precedence." In a survey conducted by Hill and Knowlton in 2004, 76 percent of Chinese college students described themselves as entrepreneurial. In 2000, the Communist Youth League and the National Student Federation conducted a survey on youth aspirations among 1,800 students in southern cities. The number one choice of these students was to be a billionaire; the second was to become a CEO of a multinational company. The students' third-most popular ideal was to be a high-ranking cadre. In short, China's students today are preoccupied with money and power—a sharp contrast with the youth of the 1980s, many of whom wanted to be China's Einstein or Mother Teresa. It is no wonder that, according to numerous surveys, Bill Gates has emerged as the most popular role model for Chinese youth. They all know he is the most successful entrepreneur and the richest man in the world. Few talk about the work of the Gates Foundation.

As pragmatists, Chinese youth pay a great deal of attention to—and demonstrate impressive skills in—cultivating networks of social relations for instrumental purposes, known as *guanxi* in Chinese. In a 2005 survey by the National Institute of Youth Studies, young participants listed interpersonal relations, career development, and income as their top three concerns, with 53 percent of them regarding interpersonal relations as the most important issue. In my own study of *guanxi* development, I have found that college students, ordinary urban youth, and young villagers alike all view friends as people who can offer substantial help. They regard a large *guanxi* network as the most important social capital one can have. The majority of young people I interviewed told me that they would be particularly careful in cultivating and maintaining good relationships with their leaders or supervisors. This practice begins at a surprisingly early age. A kindergarten teacher told me that children in her work unit routinely offer gifts to teachers during holidays; they also compare notes with peers about how to please their teachers with gifts. Follow-up interviews with parents on this topic revealed that children sometimes instruct their parents on the proper gifts. Gift giving to teachers is so common in kindergartens and primary schools that it takes considerable courage to abstain.

The presents, of course, are offered to people who are considered useful, rather than loved. And behind this increased popularity of utilitarian networks is a noticeable decline in social trust. What struck me in my research is that even children are not exempt from this—which may help to explain why youth turn out to be the least trusting cohort in Chinese society. A 2002 survey in Jinan, Shandong province, showed that the degree of social trust is lowest among those under the age of 20 and highest among those over 50 years old. In a 2006 Internet survey by Sina.com, 52 percent of respondents stated that they do not trust strangers, while 85 percent had personal experience of being cheated. It is surprising that so many of the '80ers, who are supposed to be in the most trusting age, have such a pessimistic view of social trust among unrelated people. This can only feed their pragmatism.

The Useful Cat

The most intriguing practice of youth pragmatism occurs in the domain of political participation. It is well known that the current generation of Chinese youth is apolitical—indifferent toward both official ideology and the prospect of political reforms. This distinguishes them from the young people of the 1980s, who gathered in Tiananmen Square demanding democracy and political freedom in 1989. Given this pervasive political apathy, one might expect that the Communist Party would have trouble recruiting young members—yet the reality is just the opposite. Official records of the Ministry of Education show a steady increase of young party members from 1990 to 2003. In 1990, only 0.8 percent of undergraduate students were party members. By 2003, the percentage had climbed to 3.8 percent. The most impressive growth was found among graduate students—28 percent of them were party members by 2003. The fact that more than 30 percent of college students were applying for party membership in 2003 shows that the Communist Party has no difficulty with recruitment.

In the eyes of the '80ers, there is no contradiction between their political apathy and their keen interest in party membership. Political beliefs are useless, but party membership remains valuable in today's China. Most important, it may help land a good job. From employers' point of view, party membership may indicate, more or less, that a young person is not a troublemaker. Even joint-venture or foreign-invested companies welcome students with party membership because of the expectation that they must know how to maintain good relationships with leaders.

Even among younger members of the '80er generation—those who normally would be more playful and social and less preoccupied with getting ahead—we see similar trends toward dismal pragmatism. In 2005, the Research Center of Chinese Youth conducted a nationwide survey among students of primary, middle, and high schools in both cities and the countryside. The results show that 57 percent of the students categorized their lives as unhappy because of the pressures of study, and more than 50 percent found the content of their textbooks boring or useless. Yet

58 percent of the students said they hope to earn a Ph.D., and 42 percent considered having good test scores the happiest thing in their lives. (In comparison, only 19 percent regarded "play as much as one wants" the happiest thing.)

The paradox of these students having negative feelings about academics but aspiring to do well in them reveals, once again, the utilitarian pattern of thinking and behavior among Chinese youth. They study hard because they believe high exam scores are useful, not because they are interested in the subjects; they want to obtain a doctorate because it may help them gain a good job, not because they want to commit themselves to research and teaching. In one case reported by the media in 2002, a 9-year-old girl in a southern city earned more than a dozen certificates of qualifications, covering a wide range of subjects from mathematics, history, and computer science to English and piano. To obtain these certificates on top of her regular schoolwork, she had to sacrifice all her playtime, including weekends. When asked why, she calmly told a reporter that she was working for the future because some certificates would help her become successful in the job market. Many readers were stunned by a 9-year-old planning for her future career, yet many more parents are using the girl's story as a role model for their only child.

Indeed, it is worth noting that the pragmatism of Chinese youth derives mostly from the realist teachings and practices of Chinese adults—parents, teachers, and older members of society. It is not a coincidence that the dominant ideology in China over the past 25 years has been pragmatic in nature, as reflected in the popular saying that a cat is good only if she or he can catch mice.

The roots of pragmatism did not originate with youth; they are a product of Chinese society.

Fragile Bodies, Troubled Minds

This manner of learning and living is, of course, highly stressful. The majority of China's youth find themselves constantly under pressure and anxious. In the 2005 nationwide survey, for example, 67 percent of the teenagers said they always worried about exams, and 41 percent feared they might not be able to enter a prestigious university. Surveys among college students show that some 40 percent to 45 percent of youth worry about their prospects of finding good jobs, and a small crowd begin to worry about car loans and mortgage payments even before they graduate. Most intriguingly, some of the older '80ers, who are still in their twenties, have shown concerns about being outdated and replaced by the '90ers.

These worries, fears, and anxiety about their future—along with the daily calculated efforts to move oneself ahead—take a serious toll on the health of China's youth, making many of them fragile physically. In a 2002 survey conducted among 1,000 teenagers in Shanghai's Pudong district, 21 percent of the youth said they always felt exhausted because of the pressure of study and the shortage of playtime; 61 percent reported not having enough sleep. The aforementioned 2005 nationwide survey echoed the findings in Shanghai, showing that 66 percent of primary school students and 77 percent of middle school students did not have enough sleep. When answering the question "what would you like to do if you have free time," 53 percent of the teenagers chose "to have a long and good sleep." One doctor reflected that some of his young patients were sick from sleep deprivation because they only spent about five hours in bed per night. Yet they asked the doctor to help them find a way to sleep even less so they could spend more time studying and preparing for exams.

According to statistics from the China Psychology Association, more than 10 percent of Chinese under the age of 17 do not have sound psychological health; psychologists identify heavy schoolwork, employment pressure, and a monotonous life as the major causes. The most dramatic and tragic indicator of these mental health problems is the increasingly high rate of suicide among young people. Recent studies reveal that an estimated 250,000 Chinese take their own lives every year, which translates into a suicide rate of 2 per 10,000 people, much higher than that in United States. Ranked the fifth leading cause of death among the general population, suicide is the major cause of death among China's youth. Many more youngsters have attempted or thought of suicide. A 2004 survey of 1,010 college students in the city of Wuhan, central China, reveals that 11 percent of the students had thought of committing suicide; a 2005 survey of 200 students in a Beijing college shows that 30 percent of the students had the idea.

These survey results and media reports of actual suicide cases send a clear signal about the severity of mental health issues among young Chinese, showing how fragile and stressed these young pragmatists are. To give a more concrete sense of this problem, let me cite two stories from my fieldwork in Beijing in late 2003. While investigating the social causes of child obesity, I visited the home of a 12-year-old girl who at the time weighed 140 pounds and had a hard time keeping up with basic schoolwork. She lived in a shabby one-room structure in one of the poorest neighborhoods in the city; her parents had both been laid off from state-owned enterprises. The family survived on a monthly basic stipend of 720 yuan (about $80) provided by the government to the laid-off parents. From this very tight budget, the parents took out 300 yuan every month to pay for private tutoring classes for their daughter. As a result, the family could hardly afford to buy meat except for holidays. Why tighten their belts for private tutoring? The mother told me they wanted their daughter to score high enough to get into a college, which, she insisted, was the only way that the family could lift itself out of poverty and a miserable life. Aware of her parents' high expectations and costly investment in her tutoring, the girl skipped all playtime, shortened her sleep time, and did nothing but study every day. Yet the girl's exam scores continued to drop while her body weight climbed from 92 to 140 pounds in two years.

The second story is similar, except that the family's financial situation is slightly above the average, and the focus of parental attention is a handsome young man, age 19. At the time of my research, he had failed his college exam once and was enrolled in prep school for the next year. However, he had trouble making sense of anything he was reading, constantly hearing people uttering at his back and fearing something horrible was about to happen. He would not even dare to cross a busy street without his mother leading the way. I introduced the young man to a psychologist friend, who later told me that the teenager had been under great pressure from his parents to become a successful big name ever since childhood. Yet he discovered that he could not understand his teachers' lectures in the first year of middle school and dared not let his parents know. At the same time, his parents continued to shower him with all kinds of material comforts, while urging him to study hard so that he could become rich and famous. He was at the point of mental collapse after failing the college entrance exam and had thought of killing himself several times. Thanks to the professional help, the parents eventually realized that their unreasonably high expectations and the pressures at home had damaged their son's mental health.

The frailty of the pragmatic '80ers has subjected them to social criticism in both the workplace and public life. According to a recent report on the performance of newly graduated '80ers in high-technology, media, and entertainment sectors, a large number of the young recruits lack self-discipline, are routinely late to work, and have no incentive once there to work hard. Although they are good at pleasing their bosses, they cannot take any criticism. This is mainly because, concluded the report, these self-centered youth have unrealistic high expectations about their income and position, yet they can be easily disappointed by the routine work at entrance levels. The most popular weapon of self-protection that these young professionals have used, noted by a senior personnel manager in another media report, is to quit: "They will leave whenever they are unhappy about their workplace, they will quit whenever they encounter a dip, and they can easily fall into depression and lose their direction whenever they are struck by difficulties." The '80ers, interestingly, shrug off these criticisms, saying they all result from the fact that they were lonely since childhood and thus have become more sensitive than older people.

Extra Burdens

Thus far, most scholarly and media attention on Chinese youth has focused on the young urbanites, especially college students. The reasons are obvious: urban youth are more visible to the media, more vocal when being interviewed, and easier to be surveyed. More important, urban youth have more purchasing power, spend much more than their rural counterparts on commodities beyond daily necessities, and are more open to fashion trends. In short, they are better consumers. As a 2004 "China Cool Hunt" survey report by Hill and Knowlton put it: "Imagine a population roughly the size of the Netherlands, made up of a generation of only children. Add the words 'newly rich,' 'fashion-savvy,' and 'young,' and you have just described China's millions of university students. To tap into this lucrative market, companies must first discover what these students want and how they think."

This market-driven emphasis on young urban consumers has obscured our understanding of Chinese youth as a whole because rural youth not only constitute a larger portion of the youth population but also face extra economic and social challenges in their lives. My research in rural north China shows that, as a result of the flow of information through television and other channels of mass media, plus the personal experience of rural-urban migrants, rural youth like their counterparts in the cities are exposed to market values and competition. Therefore, they have essentially the same kinds of life aspirations.

The dilemmas of individualism and pragmatism apply to rural youth as well—except that young villagers are more vulnerable and frail because they are already at the bottom of the social hierarchy under the notorious household registration system. Unlike their parents or older siblings, many rural youth now cannot bear the harsh farm work at home, and many have left to seek jobs in cities. Like most urban youth, the young villagers want to make big money quickly, to be cool and fashionable, and to become successful so they can have a comfortable life. Yet they have to endure discrimination and injustices, including extremely low wages, illegally long working hours, substandard living conditions, and police harassment and brutality. Because of the rural residency status that they were assigned at birth, they remain classified as migrant workers instead of youth even when they go to cities for work. Their joys and pain, losses and gains, love and hatred, and mental health rarely enter the sight of scholars and journalists.

There are a few exceptions, but most of them involve tragedies. In the early 1990s, for example, 87 rural youth, mostly young girls, were burned to death when they were trapped in locked factory dormitories during a fire. The personal letters left by these victims showed that they yearned for romantic love, a comfortable urban life, and a decent job that might bring them some respect. In February 2004, a 22-year-old college senior from the countryside named Ma Jiajue murdered four roommates over two days, crushing each victim's head with a hammer and hiding the body in a closet while waiting to kill the next one. Ma's anger—his roommates had accused him of cheating during a mahjong game—triggered this cold-blooded crime. He fled but was soon captured and, in June 2004, executed. After his death, what was said to be Ma's diary appeared on the Internet. From it the public learned of the economic hardship, social discrimination, and personal insults that he had endured in his short life, and the hatred that he had developed toward the privileged. Although the authenticity of this diary remains questionable, Ma has nevertheless gained sympathy and understanding posthumously. A play depicting his life story was performed in universities in May 2006, bringing to tears many audiences that thought Ma was a victim as well. His case has provoked some in the public to consider the especially difficult dilemmas that rural youth face in today's China.

The Spoiled Singleton

The frail, pragmatic, and selfish features of the new generation of youth have long been noticed and discussed by government agencies, educators, scholars, and the general public, and the most common comment is that youngsters are simply spoiled by their parents and grandparents; hence the well-known term "spoiled singleton syndrome." Many parents are worried whether these spoiled single children can shoulder all their responsibilities when they marry and have their own children, and whether they can fulfill the traditional obligation of supporting their aging parents. These concerns appear to be well justified. Indeed, an increasing number of urban youth in their twenties still have to rely on their parents for basic living because they could not find satisfactory jobs, earning them the new label of *kenlaozu*, meaning literally "those who bite their parents [for a living]." Since most urban parents can resort to pensions or other social welfare programs, many have long given up on the young generation in this respect. In rural China, however, elderly support is in a much worse state. Aging parents still have to rely on their grown children, who, being more interested in the well-being of their own nuclear families, have begun to refuse to play the traditional role.

In a sense, the catch-all diagnosis of "spoiled singleton syndrome" is misleading because it does not specify by whose standard and in what ways the singletons are spoiled. As the anthropologist Vanessa Fong has observed, Chinese parents tried their best to provide a first world material life for their single children in the context of a developing society, and they expect their children to appreciate this privilege. But, having been born in the 1980s and raised in a world of abundance—either in their own surroundings or through the media—the singleton children never feel that their material lives are excessively comfortable. And even fewer feel they were spoiled. Only when parents realize that the children take their comfortable life (at least in comparison with the parents' childhood) for granted do the parents complain the children are spoiled. Yet Chinese parents rarely recognize that this generation of teenagers and youngsters, although fed well and clothed fashionably, actually have sacrificed the carefree, purposeless, and playful part of their childhood and youthhood.

A spoiled child or youth, it might be suggested, should be innocent, full of dreams, and perhaps even idealistic because she or he has yet to learn the harsh side of reality. This is obviously not the case with the '80ers, who are arguably the most industrious laborers in the world if we take full consideration of the time they put into work—schoolwork, homework, extracurricular work, and the unnecessary or at least premature worries about their adult lives. When pushing their children for more schoolwork or teaching them to be realistic and practical, few Chinese parents spoiled the singletons. The ’80ers are fully aware of this and therefore never agree that they are spoiled. On the contrary, many feel that they already work extra hard for their parents from kindergarten through high school and therefore need to take a break when they finally become full adults—by avoiding responsibilities and refusing to play the traditional role of a filial son or daughter. In other words, behind the spoiled singleton syndrome there is the unrecognized problem of a pragmatic and stressful childhood.

The Two Faces of Youth

Putting all the pieces together, Chinese youth in the current generation come across as both individualistic fun-seekers and frail pragmatists, and I would argue that these are the two sides of the same coin. A coin, however, cannot separate its two sides, yet China’s youth do to a great degree. In the private sphere, especially when they are dealing with their parents and loved ones, they are individualistic, self-centered, conscious of rights, and bold in their pursuit of fun, the cool, and the fashionable. In the sphere of public life, on the other hand, they are bluntly pragmatic, choosing the safest way to maximize their exam scores, educational returns, income, power, and prestige. To reach these goals, they can be docile, patriotic, or aggressively competitive, depending on which tactic works best. This is why in almost all government-sponsored surveys, young people always came up with the correct answers and so are praised for knowing their rights and wrongs. This is also why many of them want to join the Communist Party while few of them believe in what the party stands for.

Although the two sides of the '80ers operate separately, one in the domain of consumption and the other in the public sphere, they do have an impact on one another. The individualistic side makes the pragmatic youth frail because they are lonely and self-centered, while the pragmatic side has turned individualistic youth cynical and immune to spiritual inspirations. Working together, the two sides drive idealism out of the current generation of Chinese youth. This should not be a surprise. The '80ers as young children had already begun to race between mathematics class and English language camps, to be reminded everyday by their parents how much investment is placed in them, and to lose sleep to fears of failing the next exam. As children, they did not have time for dreams—and the pressure to succeed has grown only more intense since. As teenagers and young adults, they lack any time for idealism.

If idealism, compassion, and naïveté are defining features of youthhood, the '80ers in China are hardly youthful. If efforts to resist and subvert the dominating ideology and symbolisms of the establishment are the core of youth culture, then China's youth hardly have a culture of their own. If the seeds of social changes are to be found in youth, then the current generation of Chinese youth is the least hopeful. As frail pragmatists, they are too wise to be naïve and idealistic and too cautious to cross any established boundaries in the public sphere.

It is unnecessary to worry that the current generation will prove unable to perform as responsible adults: their pragmatism determines that, when the time comes, they will play their expected roles properly. But I do wonder: Without young people's idealism or counterculture, where are the internal catalysts for a society to improve itself? A whole generation of pragmatic youth can be a factor for social and political stability in the short run, but in the long run they could also prove a huge liability for innovation and replenishment because there will be few to raise the bar of justice and equality or push the envelope of social progress.

Yunxiang Yan *is a professor of anthropology at the University of California, Los Angeles.*

"Is this new caste-neutral, education-hungry, spend-happy young person representative of the real India?"

India's Remix Generation

Rashmi Bansal

Winter is the season of the Big Fat Indian Wedding. My big fat Indian family recently held nuptials, attended by the usual gaggle of cousins, distantly related uncles, and faintly remembered aunts. In the midday warmth of Mumbai, we—the bride's side of the family—awaited the arrival of the groom and the traditional *baraat* (marriage procession). As a concession to modernity, he pulled up in a horse-drawn buggy, not actually astride a horse. But the bride's father was held up in one of the city's endemic traffic jams. A frantic call was placed to the groom on his cell phone: "Ask your folks to dance for a few minutes more. . . ." Pumped up on the bhangra beats of a popular Bollywood number, the celebrants hardly seemed to mind.

The scene may have appeared to be just another timeless Indian rendition of till-death-do-us-part. But scratch the surface of the traditional revelry, and a microcosm of the new India reveals itself—the cauldron that is this culture-clinging country, simmering with bubbles of energy and change. The young people in particular, the principal players in this ritual, are helping to create a fast-evolving and more Westernized but still uniquely Indian culture.

The bride and groom are both professionals. They work, in fact, at the same multinational American firm and met on the job. They are from different castes and communities—she, an Agrawal from a trader community in the northern state of Uttar Pradesh; he, a Sindhi from a former Pakistani province whose family moved to Mumbai after the 1947 partition. Yet their parents had absolutely no problem with the idea of their getting married. On the contrary, the bride's father apparently sighed in relief. Putting together an arranged marriage—where the families fix a match based on similar social backgrounds and compatible horoscopes—is no mean task today.

"Today's young women have their own ideas about the way they wish to live," the father says. The meek young women who would bow their heads and accept whatever fate handed out to them are dwindling in numbers across much of India. Economically empowered women now enter marriage with ideas of equality in their heads. "As long as the boy is well-educated and a Hindu, we are fine," is the new refrain in many urban middleclass Hindu families.

The change in attitude reflects the emergence of what amounts to a new caste—the English-speaking urban professional. These are the young men and women who strive to enter India's best technical and management universities, such as the Indian Institutes of Technology and Indian Institutes of Management. They believe that hard work and merit are what open doors to a better future. Working at large multinational or software companies, they earn more at age 24 than their government-servant fathers earned at retirement.

I saw these bright-eyed young people at the wedding. Many are from what were once derisively referred to as "small towns"—towns like Kanpur, Jaipur, Indore, and Banaras. Life there once moved at a slower pace, and does still. But the young people in the towns have taken a mental leap, thanks to satellite television and the Internet. The gap between the city-bred and the country cousins has narrowed; in some areas it has been wiped out altogether.

The girls from Kanpur were wearing sequined chiffon saris and glittering "Punjabi suits" (tunics worn with drawstring pajamas) in the style of the moment. The same department stores that were once the preserve of big cities are spreading tentacles to the towns. Malls and multiplexes are mushrooming everywhere, as corporate India wakes up to the consuming power of smaller communities. And local enterprise is not far behind. Most of the dresses at the wedding were knockoffs of styles sported on the big screen by Bollywood stars like Rani Mukherji and Preity Zinta. Bazaars today are dotted with "boutiques"—small tailoring shops run by portly women with dubious fashion design diplomas. What they lack in aesthetics training, they make up for by tuning into "India Fashion Week" and ripping off the more wearable designs.

Spend-Happy

So is God in his heaven and everything right with the country? Is this new caste-neutral, education-hungry, spend-happy young person representative of the real India? Well, yes and no. In a country as vast as India, you can never generalize. And reality depends on what side of your naan is buttered. Or whether you have naan to fill your stomach at all.

It is an inescapable fact that more than 250 million Indians, a quarter of the population, are still living officially below the poverty line—on $1 per day or less. This means they do not eat even two square meals a day. With 54 percent of India estimated to be under the age of 25, this presumably means we have more than 130 million young people who exist merely in survival mode.

The good news, however, is that the chances of upward mobility are greater than ever. And not just for the "haves." Economic data show a surge of movement into what the National Council for Applied Economic Research (NCAER) calls the "aspirer" class. These are households with an annual income between $2,000 and $4,500 a year. From 29 million households in 1996, their number has grown to 53 million (or 220 million people) today.

This kind of improvement in the standard of living over a single decade—the result of the liberalization of the economy since 1991—is unprecedented in India. And the economic reforms, including reduced state licensing for new businesses and opening up to foreign investment, have benefited no one more than India's young people. New sectors such as software services are flourishing, bringing to India the "knowledge economy" and jobs for the educated young elite. Engineering and business colleges have proliferated as more and more young people seek the all-important "professional qualification." So-called computer diplomas, offered by nationwide quickie-course chains like NIIT and Aptech, also have multiplied.

Critics of the liberalization policy—mainly on the left—contend that the fruits of this growth are not reaching the poorest of the poor. But, for the first time, it appears that even the most deprived members of society are beginning to feel the ripples of this economic tidal wave. The numbers of the "deprived" (defined by the NCAER as households earning under $2,000 a year) are projected to decline from the current 132 million households to 114 million by 2010.

So, yes, the rich in India are definitely getting richer. A new cash-rich middle class of some 60 to 80 million Indians has emerged. And the gap between rich and poor, as well as between white collar and blue collar, has grown more starkly evident. Nevertheless, things are expected to get better for more Indians than ever before.

This is especially the case with young people who have the right educational qualifications. Software giants Infosys and TCS (Tata Consultancy Services) *each* are hiring 30,000 fresh engineering graduates every year. Anyone who can speak English fluently can land a job at a call center at a starting salary of 10,000 rupees (approximately $220) per month. This may not sound like a lot, but if you are living with your parents—as many twentysomethings still do in India—the salary is essentially pocket money. With food and rent taken care of, the young employee can splurge. Thus, trainees and junior managers in offices flaunt the latest cell phones (change cycle: every six months) even while the boss sticks to a trusted old model or functional Blackberry.

Coffee shops, cinemas, Nike, Reebok, and Levis all thrive on the new let-me-spend-all-I-have young Indian. And when the young consumer needs to spend more, it is simply a matter of finding another better-paying job. With job-hopping rampant, attrition rates at companies have reached all-time highs. Indeed, in a country of more than 1 billion people, human resources managers moan about scarcity of "talent."

School-Hungry

Compounding the employers' difficulties are continuing deficiencies in India's educational system. According to the National Association for Software and Services Companies, barely 10 percent of India's annual 3 million non-technical graduates and 25 percent of its 400,000 engineering graduates are considered "employable." This is because a vast number of young Indians making their way through the abysmal state schooling system are deprived of proper primary education. Most of them study in "vernacular" (local language) schools and emerge ill-equipped to face the new, globally connected job market.

Those who can afford it send their children to so-called English medium schools. But even here, teaching methods emphasize memorization of facts and hardly any independent thinking. It is a system the British put into place, still creaking along with rewritten textbooks. The one thing it does produce is fierce competition for limited seats to the most prestigious universities.

Competition among young people is heightened further by state-supported "reservations" in colleges for students on the basis of caste, the traditional stratification of Hindu society. The "untouchables," the lowest caste, for centuries suffered discrimination and were barred from learning. The original idea behind reservations of seats in higher education and government service was to provide a form of affirmative action to lift up the lowest caste and bring its members into the mainstream of Indian society.

However, India's founding fathers envisaged a 10-year period for these reservations. Sixty years on, they persist, with no politician daring to antagonize his voting constituency by advocating their elimination. The sons and daughters of those who have already benefited from reservations corner the seats now, effectively depriving their brethren who are more genuinely in need.

In 1989, the government introduced reservations for "Other Backward Castes" (OBCs) in state jobs, taking total reservations to 50 percent of available jobs. But, unlike the untouchable castes and specified tribes, these castes were not uniformly backward. Some among them are landowners and politically powerful. Reservations thus had become more of an attempt to woo constituents along caste lines than an initiative to promote social equality. The government's action touched off a wave of student protests in 1990.

Matters came to a boil again in 2006 when the government sought to introduce OBC reservations in prestigious national universities. Young people belonging to the higher castes saw this as a direct attack on the concept of merit. Seething at the injustice, crowds of elite youths took to the streets, notwithstanding their *"khao, peeyo aur mauj karo"* ("eat, drink, and enjoy") attitude toward life, which normally leaves little time for political activism.

Medical students who spearheaded the anti-quota protest braved water cannons, sat on hunger strikes, and mobilized widespread media opposition across the country and online. The agitation split the country into two and once again brought into focus the issue of caste, which many hitherto believed was withering away.

It is interesting that the only two major student agitations in India's recent history (1990 and 2006) have been triggered by economic issues, not social injustices. In both cases, students believed that opportunities were being unfairly snatched away from them and appropriated by politicians, to be distributed according to their whim.

Resident doctors eventually called off the latest protest on the order of the country's supreme court. Student groups have filed a public interest lawsuit, but the original fire has been extinguished. Quotas are being implemented, albeit in phases. The majority is now resigned to them. The flirtation with activism having passed, young people's lives go on.

Meet the Parents

On fronts other than the economic, the young Indian—across the spectrum of class and caste—remains fairly content. And broadly conformist. The emphasis is on personal goals and achievements, but within a social and family structure.

The 1996 hit film *"Dilwale Dulhaniya Le Jayenge"* ("The Man with the Heart Will Take the Bride") hit the nail on the generational head when, unlike Bollywood lovers of yore, the movie's hero refused to elope with his lady love. A cocky young Shahrukh Khan declared he would *Coffee shops, cinemas, Nike, Reebok, and Levis all thrive on the new let-me-spend-all-I-have young Indian.* marry the lovely Kajol, but only after winning over her parents.

Parents are and will remain central characters in the young Indian's existence. The good news is that parents are adapting along with their offspring. "One has to change with the times," parents sigh, as their sons slick back their gelled hair and their daughters dump the covers-it-all *salwar kameez* for low-waist jeans and tight tee shirts.

In some matters, Indian parents have become particularly flexible. As far as consumerism or career efforts go, both parent and offspring are partners in crime. All parents want the best they can afford to give their children, especially when it comes to securing their future. This attitude ranges from the maidservant who works extra hours to send her son to an English medium school to the corporate vice president who earmarks mutual funds to support a child's future college education in America.

Of course, not all change is voluntary. Often there is simply no choice. Consider the mobile telephone, which has brought about a revolution in young India's mating manners. The vast majority of Indian parents still frown on the concept of dating. They would much prefer that their offspring hang out in groups, and certainly are not keen on the idea of "going steady." You will get distracted from your studies, they argue. Besides, sex before marriage is "against Indian culture."

So much so that every year on Valentine's Day, members of the Shiv Sena—a right-wing political party—resort to smashing up shops that sell cards, flowers, and chocolates. Party members ask couples caught holding hands in parks to pledge that they will marry. India also still has girls' hostels with ridiculous curfew times like 6:30 in the evening. None of this, of course, stops romance from blossoming.

Chatting (on the Internet), "scrapping" (communicating on the popular social networking site Orkut), and text messaging (via mobile telephone) are the three new weapons in the young woman's amour arsenal. Cell phone companies like Reliance offer "free" calls between two pre-designated numbers. The joke in college goes, if you have recently switched to Reliance from another network, you are probably head over heels in love. The mouse and the mobile have empowered the otherwise protected and constantly watched-over young Indian woman like never before.

The irony is that parents put these technologies in the hands of young people because of their perceived utility for monitoring what children are up to. Giving your son or daughter a cell phone is supposed to help you "keep in touch" and know where he or she is at any time. In fact, parents have little or no idea where their sons or daughters actually are, or whom they are speaking to. In one fell stroke, India's youth have gained a whole new world, a world featuring one thing that most everyone in this crowded country craves: privacy.

Although iPod portable music devices are still rare in India, young people find ways to tune out the world while tuning into one of their own. The sight of young people with tiny mobile-phone headphones lodged in their ears is common.

Cell phones, it should also be noted, have transcended class barriers. As of January 2007, India had 156 million mobile phone users; this includes everyone from the top to the bottom of society. Lack of a fixed address is no longer a liability. While the young man who leaves his village in search of a job may not know where he will sleep tonight, he knows that his family—or prospective employer—can reach him. The cell phone not only enables mobility; it is a new and potent symbol of a society with a spring in its step: freed of wires, free of entanglement, an India on the move.

One India

Young people, like all Indians, are in some ways divided along the lines of what has been called the "Two Indias"—the rich and the poor, the urban and the rural, the English speakers and those limited to their native tongue. In terms of culture, however, the youth of today are more unified and connected than ever before.

Not long ago, inhabitants of the south of India routinely railed against the cultural hegemony of the north. Over time, however, they have succumbed. All of India is now under the spell of Bollywood. A young lad in Chennai, the capital of the southern state of Tamil Nadu, may watch Tamilian films but also hum the catchy tune from the Bollywood blockbuster "Dhoom 2." Conversely, Tamil directors like Mani Ratnam release dubbed or reshot versions of their hit films for Hindi audiences.

Films are one unifying factor; food is another. Idlis (steaming patties of black lentils and rice) and dosa (crêpes made from a rice-and-lentil batter) from southern India are well-loved snacks in other parts of the country. Roti (unleavened bread), once unheard of in "rice country," is now often part of young people's eating-out menu in the south. Mothers jot down new recipes from televised celebrity cooking shows in a quest to offer their children more "variety."

So-called Punjabi suits have become well-entrenched all over India. With varying lengths, styles, and cuts, this versatile garment has become standard college and office wear, even in the most conservative families. But the influence of Punjab (in India's north) is seen most in music. Any song with a bhangra beat, a pop sound derived from Punjabi folk music, gets the crowd in a disco on its feet. Dancing to Hindi film songs would have been sacrilegious for the "cool" set of a previous generation. Now, party without it and you will be considered a weirdo. A recent trend that refuses to die out is the "remix" number. This is a song produced by overlaying an old and well-loved Bollywood tune with more modern and dance-happy beats.

Mix and Match

It is in some ways this remix mindset that defines young India today. Young people somehow manage to mash up the old with the new, the Indian with the Western, to produce a pop culture with a character all its own. Whether it's the pizza with paneer tikka toppings (spicy cottage cheese cubes) or traditional kurtas worn with jeans on college campuses, mix and match is the mantra.

Technology rapidly facilitates the mixing of Indian and global culture. In a country where cricket was—and still is—dominant, new sports such as Formula 1 auto racing and soccer are gaining popularity among the youth. With more than 100 channels on satellite television, *some* network will find it worthwhile to cater to a niche audience. Likewise, the Internet ensures that geography no longer limits the following of a Manchester United football club.

Economic globalization has spurred a significant change in youth's attitudes toward America. In the 1970s and 1980s, young members of the Indian elite had no qualms about migrating to the United States for "better prospects." But they retained a cynical attitude and distrust of the country. America was generally seen as an ally of India's enemy Pakistan — most noticeably during the 1971 conflict that led to the creation of Bangladesh. Russia, on the other hand, was a benefactor and friend.

That was then. In the new India, where capitalism has replaced socialism in all but name, young people see America as a country India should emulate. Microsoft founder Bill Gates is the hero of many a 16-year-old, and US car brands like Ford and Chevrolet successfully convince Indian yuppies that they can live the Great American Dream on the potholed roads of India.

But Indian culture is resilient. An underlying desire for change mingles, for example, with an abiding acceptance of fate. Indians would like better roads; they will settle now for stronger tires. Of course, young Indians are more "globalized" in the sense that they consume the same brands as their counterparts in other parts of the world, from McDonald's to MTV. These and other brands, however, have had to adapt and "Indianize" themselves. And is an MTV that plays Bollywood music 23 out of 24 hours a day really a global product?

India's youth culture contains a pleasant sense of familiarity as well as a sense of something new: one foot in the past, the other in modernity. Young people in India today still fast for God, even as they also fast for health. They will consider themselves liberal and open-minded, and yet remain deeply divided along religious lines. Hindus, who make up over 80 percent of India's population, have historically been a tolerant people. But repeated attacks by Muslim militants in cities such as Mumbai and Delhi have heightened the us-versus-them feeling. Muslims are perceived as not doing enough to suppress and punish the fanatics within their community. However, much of this is not openly expressed, and the media strive to provide a balanced view on the subject.

Respect for elders is another tradition that, surprisingly, young Indians continue to honor. They often choose not to question or resist old ways if that will "make the elders happy." Thus, Aishwarya Rai, the Bollywood star and former Miss World, consented to marry a tree because astrologers said it would help rid her horoscope of *mangal dosh* (a dangerous affliction). She did so while her fiancé, Bollywood star Abhishek Bachchan, looked on benignly.

Back at our wedding, the bride and groom performed all the usual rituals and then some. After several rounds of touching elders' feet and asking for blessings, they zipped off in a brand new Hyundai Getz. The car was a *gift* from the bride's family, we were told, not a dowry. The newlyweds might have argued about this point on their honeymoon in Switzerland. More likely, they will let age-old traditions lie and simply create new ones. "When we have a baby, you better wake up at night and change the diapers!" the bride may have cooed into her husband's ear, perhaps failing to notice the tiny headphone lodged inside it.

Rashmi Bansal *is the editor of* JAM *(www.jammag.com), a youth magazine based in Mumbai.*

"The pro-Kremlin youth movement has all the trappings of the old Young Communist League, including the creation of a cult of personality—with Putin in place of Lenin."

Conservative Vanguard? The Politics of New Russia's Youth

Thomas J. Garza

It has been a decade since Russian President Boris Yeltsin's famous dance number on the campaign trail in Rostov-on-Don. Both national and international press captured the incumbent 65-year-old energetically, if awkwardly, gyrating on stage while two young female dancers and a local rock band courted the seemingly apathetic Russian youth vote. Indeed, taking his cue from President Bill Clinton's successful use of MTV's "Rock the Vote" to woo young Americans to the polls, Yeltsin during his 1996 campaign focused considerable attention on cultivating the largest and potentially most affluent sector of the New Russia's urban population. "Vote, or you lose!" was the slogan of the day. The campaign became one in a series of efforts by the leadership to engage Russia's youth politically.

These efforts, for good and for ill, have proved fruitful. The Soviet Union's disintegration had featured two attempts by hard-liners and old-style Communists to derail the process—the first a coup in August 1991 when President Mikhail Gorbachev was vacationing in Crimea, the second a constitutional crisis in October 1993 that resulted in the Yeltsin-ordered shelling of Russia's parliament. In both instances, the crowds in the streets that stood in opposition to the old order, as well as the vast majority of casualties from the ensuing clashes, consisted primarily of Russian youth.

Likewise, Vladimir Putin's election to the presidency in 2000 resulted in no small part from the strong support he received among young voters, especially in the country's urban centers. Putin, elected at age 48, was the youngest man to lead Russia in the twentieth century and also one of the most physically fit. Frequently photographed in his karate uniform showing off his martial arts skills, Putin wooed youth with the promise of a new forward-looking generation of leadership, one that not only understood but embraced Russian energy and entrepreneurship.

Why, then, in the middle of his second term—as young people again have become the vanguard of political activity and renewed interest in the future direction of the New Russia—is Putin accused of polarizing Russia's youth?

Stray Sheep

For nearly its entire 70-year history, the Soviet Union organized youth collectively, like sheep under watch, through a sequence of what Aryeh Unger called "voluntarily compulsory" official state programs: Young Octobrists (Oktyabriata) for ages 7 to 10; Young

Pioneers (Pionery) for ages 10 to 15; and, most important, the Young Communist League (Komsomol) for ages 15 to 28. Each of these organizations provided not only uniform camaraderie and socialization, but also political and cultural indoctrination deemed necessary for a contributing member of Soviet society. Beneath the scout-like trappings of kerchiefs, campfires, and pledges were serious attempts to mold from childhood a *homo sovieticus* to populate and run the new socialist order. Throughout the cold war, contacts made in these institutions facilitated fundamental mobility through one's youth, such as getting into schools, universities, and jobs.

During the 1980s, as the Reagan-Gorbachev period of summit diplomacy reigned and the fall of the Berlin wall surprised almost everyone, Russia's own Generation X was beginning to discard the Young Pioneers' red kerchiefs and white aprons for T-shirts and Nike sneakers. Like their American post–baby-boomer counterparts described in Douglas Coupland's *Generation X,* Russia's new twentysomethings suffered from a perception of marginalization bordering on desperation.

In 1987, a groundbreaking film by the Lithuanian director Juris Podnieks, *Is It Easy to Be Young?,* chronicled the lives of Soviet youth following a Woodstock-like rock concert in 1985. The documentary gave the Soviet public—especially parents—an unprecedented account of the troubled lives of seemingly "normal" young people, revealing hooliganism, drug abuse, draft dodging, suicide attempts, and unwanted pregnancies. The film made clear that the children of the Soviet Union's "Greatest Generation" had, in the muddle of cold war propaganda and politics, become distressed, disillusioned, and disenfranchised.

The In-Crowds

By the end of the 1980s the official Soviet youth organizations began to give way to a variety of *neformaly*—unofficial nonstate youth groups based on everything from political views to musical tastes. As films, music, fashion, and other markers of Western culture began to make their way into the hands of Russia's young people, cultural tastes, rather than proscribed sociopolitical conventions, often determined the constituency of one's *tusovka*, or "in-crowd." Members of popular groups such as *stiliagi*, or "fashion victims," chose to *tusovat'sia* (hang out) with others who shared their fashion sense (thin ties, pointed shoes, narrow trousers) and musical tastes (groups such as Bravo and Sekret), while young *rokery* (bikers) preferred to listen to heavy metal (groups such as Master, Kruiz, and Aria) while working on their motorcycles.

Although these and other informal youth groups certainly had shared worldviews, politics and social reform were not their primary objectives. Yet, among some of these relatively innocuous groupings emerged more insidious collectives—factions with quite specific views on how any perestroika, or refashioning, of the country should proceed.

One of the largest of the informal groups to emerge during Mikhail Gorbachev's period of glasnost (openness) was the *afgantsy*—veterans of the disastrous war in Afghanistan begun by Leonid Brezhnev in 1980. These veterans returned to the Soviet Union deeply damaged—many of them wounded, addicted to opiates, shell-shocked, and, unlike their predecessors from the Great Patriotic War, haunted by defeat. Young veterans soon became one of the most vocal opposition groups in the last years of the Soviet Union, prompting Gorbachev to begin troop withdrawal from the region soon after his first year as Communist Party general secretary. Significantly, the *afgantsy* have remained a source of support and inspiration for the young Russians returning from the Chechen conflicts of the past 10 years.

The most notorious of the *neformaly* was a group called Liubery. These young people, predominantly male and from the Moscow suburb of Liubertsy, espoused a neofascist agenda based on the slogan "Russia for the Russians." They eschewed popular Soviet notions of a multiethnic, multinational country, and derided any influence—material or ideological—from the West.

Liubery were realistically portrayed in popular culture through films such as *My Name is Harlequin* (1988) and *A Rock and Roll Tragedy* (1988). They were even given tragicomic treatment, with tongue planted firmly in cheek, in *Sideburns*, Yuri Mamin's 1990 film about an elite Russian gang of youth who idolize the poet Pushkin and the "salvation" of Russia; and in *Luna Park* (1991), Pavel Lungin's tale of a neofascist gang whose young leader learns that his father is a Jew. The subculture received similar treatment in songs such as "My Liubertsy" by the band Lyube, and "Momma, I Love a Skinhead" by DDT.

Mockery aside, the reality and significance of the Liubery movement and other informal groups were clear to most Russians in the last days of the Soviet Union: Russia's marginalized youth were not prepared to sit quietly through the reorganization of post-Soviet Russia and let either the political old guard or new Western influences unilaterally determine the country's course into the next century. As ethnographer Hilary Pilkington suggests, the appearance of the unofficial groups became "the living embodiment of the process of democratization" during the final years of the Soviet Union.

Many of the factions represented by informal youth groups found at least some affinities with the political platforms and candidates of the 1996 presidential elections. Liubery and other nationalist groups, such as the Skinheads, supported Vladimir Zhirinovsky and his Liberal Democratic Party of Russia, or even Gennady Zyuganov's Communist Party of the Russian Federation.

It is naïve to assume that the *neformaly* simply faded away in the latter part of the 1990s and all but disappeared after 2000 with Putin's election. Since Yeltsin's election in 1996, Russia's youth have mobilized in particular around an issue that affects them directly: the Chechen war, and the military conscription required to prosecute it.

Russia for Russians

A palpable shift in youth responses to what has come to be called "Putin's war" occurred in the middle of 2003. On July 7, a small group of female Chechen terrorists strapped bombs to their bodies and attempted to detonate themselves in the middle of a Kryl'ya (Wings) rock concert. One woman succeeded, killing 21 and wounding 60 in the crowd of more than 20,000 mostly Russian concertgoers. Because the venue was a rock concert, the vast majority of attendees were younger than 30, just like the majority of Russians fighting in Chechnya.

The Kryl'ya bombing not only ripped through the grounds of the Tushino airfield where the concert was held. It also split the allegiances of many Russian youth into two divergent political camps: one of antiwar, anti-Putin liberals; the other, a larger movement of nationalist xenophobes.

Combined with deadly attacks on Russians in Moscow's Dubrovka Theater in 2002, and at a school in Beslan in 2004, the bombing helped fuel the reemergence of a patriotic pro-government "Russia for the Russians" youth organization. In spite of this group's progressive sounding name, Moving Together (Idushchie vmeste), its members vow to use "any means necessary" to combat what they perceive as a growing threat to the future of Russia after Putin finishes his second term in 2008.

The threat, in their view, comes from the young liberal revisionists who would prefer to see an end to the Chechen war, the establishment of an independent Russian media, and more transparency in the government. With a reported membership of more than 75,000, Moving Together claims to be grooming 5,000 "commissars" to assume positions within the Russian government over the next four years.

The conservative group has held massive rallies to support Putin's policies, performed pop songs about the president, and destroyed books by modern Russian authors. Russian-born writer Gary Shteyngart has commented that the pro-Kremlin youth movement has all the trappings of the old Young Communist League, including the creation of a cult of personality—with Putin in place of Lenin.

In an example of its zeal for acting as Russia's new morality police, Moving Together charged Russian writer Vladimir Sorokin with purveying pornography in his novel *Gay Blue Lard.* (It includes a fictional depiction of a sexual encounter between Stalin and Khrushchev.) Sorokin, along with Viktor Pelevin and Venedikt Erofeev, is very popular with Russia's so-called *"zolotaia molodezh',"* or "golden youth"—the educated youth of privilege who are frequent objects of attack by Moving Together members.

Nashi (Ours), a pro-Putin group spun off from Russia's right-wing youth movement in early 2005, claims political independence from the Kremlin. The moniker "Ours" is a particularly insidious one. Not only does it invoke like-minded "folk like us," it carries the added connotation of nationalism, implicitly referring to an eponymous documentary that positively portrayed police violence in the Baltic states aimed at quelling movements for national independence. Over the past two years, Nashi has been visibly active throughout Russia, restoring war memorials and churches, volunteering in old people's homes, and picketing orphanages that permit foreign adoption of Russian children.

Meanwhile, as foreigners and the commodity trappings of Western consumerism have become more common, especially in the larger cities, informal youth gangs have expressed their animosity by physically attacking those perceived as alien—especially people of African or Asian origin and anyone considered "dark," including native Russians of Georgian, Armenian, Chechen, or Azerbaijani ethnicity.

Lemons and Apples

In 2004, the youth branch of the liberal Yabloko party formed its own organization. In response to Moving Together's seemingly reflexive pro-Putin stance, the new group chose Moving Without

Putin as its name. Ilya Yashin, its 23-year-old leader, claims the current administration stifles any new political life and prevents ordinary citizens from becoming involved in meaningful policy debate. Renamed Defense (Oborona) in 2005, the group protests what it calls the censorship, bureaucracy, and propaganda of the Putin administration. During its first antigovernment rally in April 2005, authorities made several arrests, allegedly in response to overt calls for civil war in Russia.

Lenses on the Chechen War

Numerous films have documented the skeptical and evolving attitudes of Russia's young people toward the wars in Chechnya. Most of these movies not only concern youth, but are produced and directed by young filmmakers. Sergei Bodrov's *Prisoner of the Caucasus* (1996) revived nineteenth-century awe and sympathy toward the Caucasus through the eyes of Zhilin, a young and handsome Russian recruit (portrayed by the late Sergei Bodrov, Jr.), in the context of the 1994 Russo-Chechen war. Zhilin finds himself torn between his loyalty to Russia and his heart, which finds sympathy for a young Chechen girl. Meanwhile, Zhilin's mother tries to secure his freedom by negotiating directly with a Chechen warlord in an authentic portrait of the growing sentiment and impact of the antiwar group the Union of the Committees of Soldiers' Mothers of Russia.

After the second Chechen war erupted in 1999, Aleksei Balabanov's *The War* (2002) deromanticized the conflict with a harsh portrait of both sides. The film's young narrator is a captured Russian computer specialist who negotiates deals between Chechen warlords and the representatives of two captured British actors. Balabanov is also the director of the popular films *Brother* (1997) and *Brother 2* (2000), which depicted the complex character of Danila Bagrov, a disillusioned soldier who goes AWOL from basic training during the Chechen war. Trained in the construction of explosive devices, and with a passion for the music of the antiwar rock group Nautilus Pompilius, Danila uses his military survival skills to combat the new enemy—the Chechen mafia—in St. Petersburg in order to save his brother.

As the brooding young man of action, Danila—played by Bodrov—became a hero of Russian youth at the turn of the millennium by dealing with the demands of the New Russian order (which include conscription), while trying to look after Russian society's marginalized fringes. When he died in an avalanche accident while filming in the Caucasus in 2004, Bodrov was virtually canonized by Russian youth—much like Viktor Tsoy, the front man of the rock group Kino, who died in a car accident in 1990. Both men, each in his time, demonstrated that Russian youth could manipulate the system and ultimately be successful.

Of particular note among Chechen war films is Andrei Konchalovsky's *House of Fools* (2003), which blurred the usual black-white ethnic line between Russians and Chechens. *House of Fools* depicts the lives of patients in a mental institution in southern Russia near the Chechen border who try to cope with their own issues on top of the war raging around them. This time, though, just who is the ethnic "Other" is unclear: many of the patients are Russified Chechens; others are Muslim Russians; and the main love interest involves the heroine falling in love with and briefly marrying a Chechen rebel.

In the midst of a fight for an incomprehensible objective, a young commanding officer of Russian troops becomes so shell-shocked that he begins to reduce the entire conflict to his disgust over his mud-caked boots. Unlike *The War, House of Fools* allows the humanity of those living through the conflict to prevail, albeit in an insane asylum, supporting the notion that the "fools" now run the place and the sane people are in the asylum. Although the young Russian commander—delirious from the carnage around him—curses the Chechens, wishing all of them dead, he recants his curse as the effects of a morphine injection take over, wishing instead an end to the war.

Ours and Theirs

Television, too, has played no small part in contributing to the reinvention of post-Soviet youth, especially in light of the Chechen war and the rise of organized crime in Russia. In 2003 and 2004, *The Brigade* aired as a 16-part made-for-television series chronicling the lives of five Russian schoolmates who form a lifelong bond after one returns from his service in the Russian army just before the Soviet Union's disintegration. The men form an alliance and swear eternal loyalty to each other and begin a life of crime as Moscow and Russia enter into the age of Yeltsin's new capitalism. Indeed, the growth of organized crime in Russia was spurred by both the Soviet Union's collapse and the subsequent venture into Chechnya. For many disenfranchised post-Soviet youth, the mob represents essentially a job opportunity, certainly preferable to continued service in the military.

The Brigade presents organized crime as the new imperial power in Russia—supported by the frequent use of colonial language.

Mob bosses talk of their territory, of receiving dues from clients, and of one group invading the other's turf. But most significant is the overlay of the excesses of consumerism on the young characters in the New Russia and the emphasis on material acquisition and exploitation. As the gang (or "brigade") acquires more power and influence, it finds itself in competition with the legitimate Russian government for control over cash industries, such as the drug trade and arms sales.

Thus, our young Russian hero, not accidentally named Sasha Belov (White), decides that his gang should help the Chechens beat the Russian forces so that he and his brigade can keep local control. In one episode, we see director Aleksei Sidorov's obvious framing of blue eyes to indicate the "good guys" executing the sabotage of a delivery of Russian arms to a Chechen military outpost. The series uses constant overt racial profiling to inform the (Russian) viewer who is "ours" and who is "theirs" among the characters.

The portraits of Russian young people are varied and constantly changing: one moment they are former soldiers who had defended the Motherland against the enemy; the next they are entrepreneurs who keep Russia and its oil resources independent from Western opportunists; then they are a new generation of aspiring politicians striving to serve the common Russian's interests.

The Brigade emphasizes the underlying duplicity of Russians fighting in the Chechen war—but not on the front lines. The Chechens, meanwhile, are not presented as treacherous. The borders of the perceived Chechen Republic define who is their enemy; only when that border is violated do they act defensively.

"They're Already Here"

Taken together, these ambivalent portraits in films and television reflect a complex split in attitudes among Russia's youth toward the war. While the first incursion into Chechnya in 1994 galvanized an anti-conscription sentiment among young people (and many other Russians as well), once the war hit closer to home, including attacks on Russian civilians, the tide of nationalism turned. Liberal antiwar groups, wanting an end to both the conflict and the conscription, remain active. But far more prevalent are nationalistic, right-wing pro-government youth groups that fully support Putin's war.

A few days after the 2003 bombing of a rock concert in Moscow, the popular news weekly *Zhurnal* posted a grim cover photo of the torso of a young Chechen *shakhidka,* one of the so-called Black Widow suicide bombers. She was shown dressed entirely in black with a homemade bomb taped around her waist. Published next to the photo were three words that resonated with Russians' new attitude toward their war on terror: *"Oni uzhe zdes'"*—"They're already here." They, not we; already, not later; here, not there. Interestingly, both sides of the Russian youth movement have used this image in their propaganda: one as a cry for peace, the other as a call to arms. *T. J. G.*

Yet another youth group, It's Time! (Pora!), led by Andrei Sidelnikov, has taken its cue from the successful youth-led street protests of the Orange Revolution in Ukraine, which ultimately brought Viktor Yushchenko to power in 2005, and from the earlier successful efforts of the Serbian student organization Resistance (Otpor), which unseated Slobodan Milosevic in 2000. It is not coincidental that the youth resistance movement in Ukraine was also called Pora! Both of these earlier youth movements used live rock music to attract participants to street protests and to lend a rhythm and lyric slogans to their protest chants. Such tactics are reminiscent of the earlier glasnost period of Russian reformists in the late 1980s who rallied behind the lyrics and unrelenting beat of songs like Tsoy's "I Want Change!" with the band Kino.

The Kremlin, however, was quick to respond to the attempts by It's Time! to use rock music as both a draw and a message for Russian youth. In March 2005, Putin's deputy chief of staff and political strategist, Vladislav Surkov—not incidentally a former songwriter for the rock band Agata Kristi—met with eminent members of Russia's music industry, including Boris Grebenschikov of the rock band Akvarium. The meeting was supposedly convened to discuss topics ranging from piracy to the propensity to put *popsa* (mindless pop music) on Russian television and radio. In reality, media leaks indicated that the Kremlin was seeking to gain and cultivate the music industry's support, or at least persuade it to remain neutral, in the event of public protests or large-scale gatherings.

As is often the case in Russia, politics makes for odd alliances; the youth movements are no exceptions. Given Nashi's pro-Putin rhetoric and nationalist agenda, the left has embraced alliances with virtually any other youth organization that is anti-Putin, including the National Bolshevik Party, led by former Soviet writer in exile turned anti-Western propagandist Eduard Limonov. During the 2003 Russian Duma elections, the Yabloko youth organization and the National Bolsheviks led joint protests, prompting Putin aide Surkov to comment that a "fifth column" of leftists and rightist radicals had emerged, with lemons (referring to Limonov) and apples (referring to the Yabloko party) growing on the same branch.

The lock-step agreement of Nashi with the Putin administration has recently reached new levels of public demonstration. Following the July 2006 assassination of Shamil Basayev, the Chechen terrorist leader who claimed responsibility for both the Dubrovka Theatre and the Beslan school sieges, the pro-Putin prime minister of Chechnya, Ramzan Kadyrov, was invited to visit the youth group's headquarters. During his tour, Kadyrov reportedly called for a Duma resolution to allow Putin to serve a third term, suggesting that he needed 10 years to finish his work in the Chechen republic.

The Kremlin continues to deny any official affiliation with Nashi, but Surkov was clearly one of its principal initiators, and since 2005 Putin himself has met often with other organizers of the group. According to numerous reports, in addition to several million dollars in support from the Kremlin, Nashi has received funding from Gazprom, the state-controlled energy corporation.

Other youth organizations continue to represent minority political parties, reminiscent of the 1996 presidential election. Groups such as the Avant-garde of the Communist Youth, a radical-left organization led by 25-year-old Aleksandr Shalimov, and the Locals (Mestnye), a "green" environmental group, all add to a renaissance of youth interest in political affairs. Overall, however, the conservative pro-Putin organizations, led by Nashi, outnumber the antigovernment groups by more than three to one and have, according to unofficial estimates, more than 10 times the membership.

Popsa and Politics

Over the past decade, various Russian media have also become more active in promoting and catering to the youth population, particularly in its consumerist role—but not exclusively.

The print media targeting Russia's teenybopper set (ages 11 to 15) are indistinguishable from comparable magazines in the United States and Europe, featuring titles such as *Cool, Cool Girl, Peer,* and *Bravo.* Mindless articles about film stars, horoscopes, grooming tips, and inoffensive advice on getting through puberty fill these magazines. Journals targeting older Russian youth, however, are considerably more sophisticated. The glossy print youth press since 1996 has been decidedly liberal. Magazines such as *Ptiuch* and *OM* promote a culture of Russian youth that is fashionable, intelligent, and decidedly upwardly mobile. Both magazines depict the urban youth scene through reviews of films, books, clubs, and restaurants, as well as of politicians and contemporary writers.

There is certainly no dearth of frivolous *popsa* on contemporary Russian radio and music television stations, featuring interchangeable boy bands (such as Ivanushki International, Primier Ministr, and Smash) and girl groups (including Strelki, Blestiashchie, and Via-Gra), as well as quasi-intellectual bands with thin veneers of social commentary, such as the faux-lesbian duo Tatu and the angst-driven St. Petersburg group Splin. As if to validate Russia's place in world pop music, the runner-up in the 2006 Eurovision Song Contest was Dima Bilan, with a soupy but energetic rendition of an English-language song, "Never Let You Go."

Even so, as the political "revolutions" in Serbia, Ukraine, and Georgia demonstrated, issue-driven pop and rock music can play a significant role in galvanizing and mobilizing cadres of young citizens and voters. The situation in Russia is proving to be no different. With popular bands such as B-2 releasing patently antiwar recordings such as "The Uncounted Soldier" ("Nechetnyi voin") in 2006, and many other artists lending their music to films critical of Putin's domestic policies, there is a steady increase in the use of popular media directed at provoking political consciousness among Russia's youth.

"Don't Touch This"

The months preceding Basayev's assassination in July were relatively quiet ones in the ongoing war in Chechnya. The Group of Eight summit in St. Petersburg this summer drew attention to Russia's rising international stature and continuing economic growth. Today, in the charged atmosphere of disparate groups vying for the allegiance of Russia's youth, growing numbers of twentysomethings frequent the proliferating coffee houses and Internet cafés that dot city streets.

The nation's educational system and employment market are slowly emerging from post-Soviet collapse and becoming more responsive to young people's needs. As a result, the sense that young urban Russians are seeing their futures in the New Russia rather than jockeying for jobs abroad appears to be growing—at least for now. This sentiment was popularized in a 2006 film, *Piter FM,* in which an intelligent, upwardly mobile young architect turns down a contract to live in Berlin and opts to stay in Russia.

Russia today is demographically troubled. Indeed, Putin this year offered cash incentives and tax relief to couples who have more than one child. Yet Russian youth, ages 18 to 30, are still a growing segment of the urban population. And political organizations are not the only groups to target this audience. In the current mood of economic boom, spurred by rising oil prices and increasing energy demand, Russian marketers also have taken note of the youth population—and its increasingly disposable income.

Following the Soviet Union's disintegration, young people at first seemed to grasp at anything with a foreign label for status and prestige. Now they are becoming more discerning consumers. In Moscow, new stores such as Respublika accommodate the developing tastes of Russian youth in books, art, and music recordings. In late 2005, a new 24-hour cable television channel, O_2 TV, was inaugurated, catering exclusively to young Russians. The channel, which is available in more than 160 Russian cities and has 14 million subscribers, warns its viewers, "You are what you watch." It operates in tandem with a sophisticated interactive website (<http://www.o2tv.ru>), which features live chatrooms, blogs, and streaming videos, all aimed at an increasingly technology-savvy younger generation.

A popular 2003 poster by the Russian graphic artist Bukheevy depicts the slogan *"Ne Trozh' Molodezh',"* a slang expression meaning "Don't Touch the Youth." The graphic for the slogan exaggerates the syllable "ezh" (hedgehog) in *"Molodezh'"* (youth), suggesting that Russia's youth can be tough and prickly when provoked. (In Russian folklore, the hedgehog is an enduring symbol of nature, enjoying life—so long as it is left undisturbed.)

Whether perceived as advice or a warning, the slogan is an apt one, as globalization simultaneously propels Russia into the twenty-first century socially and culturally, while widening gaps economically and politically among its citizens. The Putin government's policies—particularly in Chechnya, where decisions palpably affect young Russians—have simultaneously mobilized and polarized the youth, provoking them into political activism. This activism has transcended the cause of the Chechen war and moved, through the formation of new youth groups, into a broader spectrum of political and social concerns.

As Russians look toward the 2008 elections and consider their country's future, it seems evident that young people will play a substantial role in deciding both. Whether in the service of promising or ominous outcomes, of liberal reform or nationalist chauvinism, the involvement of youth in Russian politics must be considered a plus, if only because it enlarges the scope of civic participation.

Thomas J. Garza *is an associate professor and director of the Center for Russian, East European, and Eurasian Studies at the University of Texas at Austin.*

"In the first half of the twentieth century, Europeans went from childhood to adolescence to young adulthood, and they reached a settled young adulthood by their early 20s. No more."

The Long and Leisurely Route: Coming of Age in Europe Today

Jeffrey Jensen Arnett

Marie, age 28, is a student at a university in Denmark, studying psychology. Currently she is in Italy, collecting interviews for a research project, and living with her Brazilian boyfriend Pablo, who is studying engineering there. Her plan is to become a psychologist who works with deaf children and their families, but much of her life is up in the air right now. How much more education should she pursue, if any? She and Pablo would like to marry and have two children eventually, but when? Their lives are busy now. How could they fit children in amid their other ambitions and adventures?

If there is one thing that is certain about Marie's existence, it is that her life is vastly different from that of her mother or grandmother when they were 28 years old. Just 50 years ago, all over Europe, the median marriage age was in the early 20s. For most young couples, the first child came about a year after marriage, and was soon followed by another, with many couples going on to have three or four children. Few young people received education past their mid-teens. By the mid-20s, the typical European was well settled into adult roles, with respect to both work and family.

Then, quite suddenly and unexpectedly, the typical path from the late teens through the 20s changed. First came the introduction of the birth control pill, in the early 1960s, which made it relatively easy for young people to begin their sexual lives in their teens without the fear of an unintended pregnancy. Premarital sex soon became common and widely accepted as the norm. Also, the economy's basis changed from manufacturing to information and technology, and the new economy led more and more young people to pursue more and more education, often well into their 20s. The median marriage age rose steadily and soon became higher than ever before. It is now nearly 30 in most of Western Europe, and still rising. Age at first childbirth became steadily later as well, and now instead of having three or four children most Europeans have two, or one, or none at all. The total fertility rate across Europe is now just 1.4 children per woman.

In sum, over a period of just a few decades, from the early 1960s to the present, the lives of young people in Europe (as in other industrialized countries) have changed so dramatically that a new period of the life course has been created. In the first half of the twentieth century, Europeans went from childhood to adolescence to young adulthood, and they reached a settled young adulthood by their early 20s. No more. Today, young people in Europe go from childhood to adolescence to what I have called "emerging adulthood," before they enter young adulthood. For most people, emerging adulthood lasts from the late teens until the late 20s.

Europe is diverse, of course, and there are important differences between east and west, and north and south, as well as within countries according to social class and ethnic group. But it is nevertheless possible to paint with broad strokes an overall picture of what characterizes emerging adulthood in Europe today. On the basis of my research into the phenomenon generally, I have concluded that five main features distinguish emerging adulthood from the adolescence that precedes it and the young adulthood that follows it. Emerging adulthood is the age of identity exploration, of instability, of focusing on one's self, of feeling in-between, and of possibilities. All of these features can be found in the experience of young Europeans.

Pursuing the Ideal

First, emerging adulthood is the age of identity exploration. This means it is a time of finding out who you are and what kind of adult life you want to pursue, mainly in terms of love and work. In the course of emerging adulthood, young people explore possibilities and move closer to making enduring choices in both of these areas. With respect to love, most emerging adults have involvements with a series of love partners. In contrast to adolescence, when love relationships are mainly for fun and recreation, during emerging adulthood love relationships are usually entered with the underlying question: Is this the kind of person who would be a good partner for me for life? In northern (but not southern) Europe, one way of answering this question is through cohabitation. The majority of northern Europeans now cohabit with at least one partner before marriage. In both north and south, the goal is to find not merely a reliable marriage partner but a "soul mate," someone who provides an ideal complement to one's own identity.

With respect to identity exploration and work, emerging adulthood is a period of trying out a series of educational and occupational paths in search of a job that provides an ideal identity fit. In work as in love, expectations are high. The goal is not to find a mere job but a job that is self-fulfilling, enjoyable, and personally satisfying—in short, a job that is an expression of one's identity.

This issue has special meaning with respect to Europe's educational systems. Although there is variation within Europe, in most countries across the continent a crucial decision has to be made at age 14 or 15, in choosing which type of secondary school to enter. Will it be a university preparatory school, or a business school that provides preparation for jobs such as accounting, or a trade school that teaches skills for jobs such as plumber and electrician? Once this choice is made, it is difficult to change tracks later. This system, however, was developed over a century ago, when the meaning and purpose of work were quite different—that is, when the purpose of work for almost everyone was simply to provide for one's self and family. Now that the goal of work is identity fulfillment, the old system is incompatible with emerging adults' desires to try different educational and occupational paths until they find the one that provides the right identity match. The clarification of one's identity is something that takes place today primarily in emerging adulthood, not in adolescence.

Consequently, today one can observe a growing tension between European governments and emerging adults. The governments wish to discourage emerging adults from changing tracks once they have entered one. The longer emerging adults stay in the educational system, and the more often they change educational paths, the longer they constitute budget liabilities to the government, rather than taxpaying workers. However, emerging adults increasingly experience the old system as intolerably rigid and inflexible. As their identities become clearer in their late teens and perhaps early 20s, they seek to change educational and occupational paths to match their identity needs, and they press their school officials and governments to allow them to do so. European systems are growing more flexible in response to the demands of emerging adults, but governments give this ground reluctantly for financial reasons.

A Time of Stress

A second feature of emerging adulthood is that it is the age of instability. In the course of their identity explorations, emerging adults frequently change directions. Finding a soul mate and identity-based work is a tall order. These goals are elusive, and in their pursuit of them emerging adults change love partners and change jobs and educational directions.

This instability, in most of Europe, is reflected in residential changes. In southern Europe, most emerging adults stay at home into their late 20s, and many young men stay home even into their early 30s. However, in northern and eastern Europe, the typical pattern is to leave home in the late teens, following secondary school. For the next decade many residential changes follow: moving in with a roommate, moving out when the roommate becomes tiresome, moving in with a romantic partner, moving out when the relationship sours, moving within their country or to a different country within Europe (or perhaps to the United States) for a period of educational training, an occupational opportunity, or simply a travel adventure.

It is the instability of emerging adulthood that sometimes makes it a difficult period. For most emerging adults, their late teens and 20s are a time of high well-being and optimism (more on this below). However, the frequent changes that emerging adults experience can be stressful. Changing love partners can be exciting, but it can also be unpleasant, especially when one is the recipient rather than the initiator of the change. Similarly, emerging adults change jobs and educational directions in search of new opportunities, but each change requires an adjustment that may be stressful.

In Europe, an especially notable source of instability during emerging adulthood is unemployment. Rates of unemployment in Europe are typically about twice as high for emerging adults as for other adults, and are especially high in southern Europe. The experience of losing a job, or of striving to find employment yet being unable to do so, is frustrating and demoralizing for emerging adults. For example, one study in six European countries reported high rates of psychological distress among emerging adults who were unemployed. In a follow-up study six months later, the distress had eased only for those who had found a full- or part-time job or had gone back to school.

The Apex of Freedom

A third feature of emerging adulthood is that it is the self-focused age. By this I mean that emerging adulthood is the time in the entire life course when people are most free from institutional demands and obligations. Children and adolescents have to attend school daily, and the rest of their daily lives is structured by their parents and other adults. Beyond emerging adulthood, most adults' lives are structured by obligations to employers, love partners, and children. In emerging adulthood, people have more freedom to decide for themselves how to live than they have ever had before or will ever have again.

One distinctively European form that the self-focused age takes is the increasing pervasiveness in Europe of a "gap year" between the end of secondary school and the beginning of university or other postsecondary education. During their gap year emerging adults often travel to other European countries or the United States, for a vacation or to work. Or, they may stay at home and simply have a year or two of working in temporary jobs and having fun with their friends.

Of course, it has long been true that some young Europeans have been unencumbered and footloose during their 20s. In Europe during the nineteenth century, at the height of Romanticism, there was an ideal, especially in Germany, of young men having a *wanderschaft* or *wanderjahr,* that is, a period in their late teens or early 20s that would be devoted to travel and self-exploration before settling into adult commitments. Similarly, in Britain many upper-class young men enjoyed a "continental tour" or "grand tour" of Europe before entering long-term adult roles.

These experiences, however, were reserved mainly for the elite, and solely for young men (young women would not have been allowed to travel without a chaperone). What is different today is that the opportunity to experience a self-focused period between adolescence and young adulthood, perhaps including travel, is available to a much broader range of young people in Europe, and to young women as well as young men. The gap year is a classic example of emerging adulthood as the self-focused age. It is the kind of experience that is only possible in emerging adulthood.

"Self-focused," incidentally, should not be confused with selfish or egocentric. Emerging adults are notably *less* egocentric than adolescents are, considerably better at taking the perspective of others. This is one of the reasons most of them get along much better with their parents than they did as adolescents. They learn to understand their parents as persons, with goals and needs much like their own, and so they judge them less harshly.

On the Way but Not There Yet

The fourth feature of emerging adulthood is that it is the age of feeling in-between. Most people from their late teens to their mid-20s feel they are neither in adolescence nor adulthood but somewhere in between. This is in part what led me to the term "emerging adulthood," because I believed this term described well their feeling of being on the way to adulthood but not there yet. These findings were surprising to me and many others a decade ago, but they have now been replicated and extended many times in the United States, across social classes, regions, and ethnic groups. Highly similar findings have also been reported by now in South Korea, Australia, Argentina, Israel—and in countries all over Europe. Feeling in-between is a remarkably pervasive feature of emerging adulthood. It is not until about age 30 that most people report feeling fully adult.

Equally surprising are the criteria that young people in Europe (as in the United States) now use to mark the entry into adulthood. Traditionally, marriage has been regarded as the definitive marker of adulthood. Across a wide range of cultures around the world, marriage has had the connotation not only of joining together a man and a woman in a lifelong bond, but also of marking the marriage partners' rise to status as adult members of the community. Now, however, studies all over Europe and in other countries show that marriage no longer denotes adult status. In interviews that ask open-ended questions, it is almost never mentioned as a criterion for adulthood. And in questionnaire surveys that offer various possible milestones for indicating adulthood, it repeatedly ends up close to rock bottom in importance. The same low rating has been found for other traditional criteria such as finishing school, starting full-time work, and having a child.

If not the traditional markers, then what today signifies adulthood for young Europeans? The most important markers of adulthood now are *individualistic,* mainly these three: accepting responsibility for one's self, making one's own decisions, and becoming financially independent. A clear shift is evident from markers measured externally by the community, such as marriage and finishing school, to markers measured internally by the self, such as accepting responsibility for oneself and making independent decisions.

Aiming High

Fifth and finally, emerging adulthood is the age of possibilities. It is a time of life when hopes run high, because few doors have been firmly closed and all dreams still seem alive. Emerging adults' dreams are usually different from the dreams of children and adolescents. Emerging adults rarely dream of being a movie star, or a rap star, or a professional athlete. Instead their dreams are more down-to-earth: a soul mate for life, and work that is enjoyable and pays well and maybe even does some good in the world. Even if life is difficult in the present for emerging adults—as it often is, since their jobs often do not pay very well and the search for a soul mate can be frustrating—nearly all of them believe that eventually life will be kind to them, and they will attain at least some semblance of their dreams.

I developed this theory on the basis of my research with Americans, and some readers may think now that this sounds very American, the idea of emerging adulthood as the age of possibilities. Americans are well-known for their optimism, perhaps because their country has not been the battlefield for the world's worst wars, as Europe has. However, the same high hopes that I found among American emerging adults I also found among emerging adults in Denmark, and Danes are hardly known for their sunny spirits.

It may be that emerging adults in the United States are optimistic not because they are American, but because they are young—which is why young Europeans share their optimism. As Aristotle observed long ago, dreams are cheap among the young because their dreams have not yet been tested in the fires of real life. We adults know all too well the things that can go wrong in the course of adult life because we have experienced them or seen them happen to people whom we know and love. But in the world of the young, during the age of possibilities, it seems that no one is going to end up experiencing a bitter divorce, and no one is going to end up in a dead-end job they hate, and no one is going to suffer from alcoholism, or a terrible accident, or a financial disaster, or chronic mental or physical illness, or an early death. Everyone will find a lifelong partner, and a great job, and live happily ever after.

The Restless and the Excluded

It is, of course, important to recognize that not everyone in Europe enjoys equal access to the freedom and opportunities of emerging adulthood. Compared to the rest of the world today, and any part of the world in the past, European states have been marvelously successful in spreading the affluence of their societies so that the great majority is middle class, with only a small proportion of rich and poor. This generalized affluence is an important condition for emerging adulthood, because remaining in education into one's 20s and then searching for identity-based work are luxuries that are possible only if it is not necessary to find a job, any job, from an early age in order to help one's family survive.

Most young Europeans enjoy the benefit of this general affluence and experience a long and leisurely emerging adulthood, but there remain areas that are struggling economically—for example, southern Italy, parts of northern Great Britain, and some of the countries of Eastern Europe such as Romania and Albania.

In these areas, economic pressures are greater and consequently the freedoms and opportunities of emerging adulthood are restricted. All over Europe, as in the rest of the industrialized world, education is the key to occupational opportunities, and whoever receives relatively little of it is likely to struggle in emerging adulthood and beyond. The manufacturing jobs that formerly provided wellpaying (if also tedious and often dangerous) work for working-class men are scarcer than in the past and growing scarcer every day.

At the same time, it is important not to overstate the influence of social class on emerging adulthood in Europe. Because of the generosity of the European welfare state, combined with tax systems designed to redistribute wealth across the population, the range of social class differences is narrower in most European countries than it is in the United States, which may result in fewer differences between emerging adults of different social classes. Having interviewed both middle-class and working-class emerging adults in the United States and Denmark, I have been struck by their similarities more than their differences. Across groups, they seek a soul mate and self-fulfilling work, and during their emerging adult years they hope to have some self-focused fun.

Perhaps more important than the class issue in Europe is the issue of immigrants. In recent decades many have come to Western European countries hoping to obtain the benefits of their affluent and well-functioning societies. Some came originally as "guest workers" to do the sorts of jobs that affluent Europeans prefer not to do; others have come as refugees from unstable, war-torn parts of the world. Now the children of many of these immigrants are reaching emerging adulthood, and, because they have grown up in European societies, their expectations and aspirations for their lives are similar to those of other young Europeans.

However, as they pursue educational and occupational opportunities during this time in their lives they frequently find doors barred to them because of racial and ethnic discrimination. Resentment and rage often follow—and sometimes riots, as with the young Muslims in France in 2006. This response in turn generates further discrimination, increasing the urgency for solutions to break the cycle that have so far proved elusive.

The Cause of a Crisis?

Recognizing the development over the past 50 years of emerging adulthood as a new period of the life course illuminates a variety of issues, among them Europe's demographic problem. The continent has too many old people and not enough young ones. Worse yet, with each year there are more and more old ones and fewer and fewer young ones. Life expectancy is steadily increasing, but young people are not having enough children to sustain the population at its current level. Not one country in Europe—north or south, east or west—has a birth rate that reaches the replacement rate of 2.1 children per woman. In the countries of southern and eastern Europe the birth rate is especially low, barely one child per woman. If this pattern continues in the decades to come, it will make the welfare states of Europe extremely difficult if not impossible to sustain.

This is a well-known problem. Less well-known is how the development of emerging adulthood is a fundamental cause of it.

Low fertility rates have multiple causes, of course, but one important cause appears to be that young Europeans have grown accustomed to the fun and freedom of emerging adulthood. Many find themselves reluctant to give up this lifestyle once they reach age 30 even as more of their peers are moving into family responsibilities. A recent survey in Germany found that one-fourth of German men in their late 20s had no intention of ever having children. The main reason they gave for this decision was that they did not want to be bound by that responsibility. That is, they prefer to continue to live the self-focused life they have come to enjoy in the course of emerging adulthood.

Further insights on emerging adulthood and fertility in Europe come from recent ethnographic work by Carrie Douglass of Mary Baldwin College, along with her colleagues. They are anthropologists who set out to investigate the human experience behind the European trend of lower fertility rates. In exploring the larger question of how the nature of young people's lives has changed now that they no longer devote their 20s to marriage and caring for young children, the researchers unearthed a great deal of fascinating and important information on emerging adulthood.

Douglass and her colleagues describe the diversity that persists in Europe, but the consistent theme across countries is that young people want to enjoy a period of freedom and independence between adolescence and adulthood. In Norway, for example, most young people want to have children eventually, but they have set a number of prerequisites that must first be fulfilled: to live independently for some years, to finish their education, to be settled in a job, and to have lived with a partner for some time. There is also the expectation that the 20s will include a period devoted to travel or some other self-focused, self-developing activity. There is a clear social norm that emerging adulthood "should" be enjoyed for some years before parenthood is entered.

Douglass's own ethnographic research in Spain provides a complementary example from southern Europe. In recent decades the median marriage age in Spain has risen to nearly 30 and the fertility rate has plunged to among the lowest in the world despite a strong cultural tradition of large extended families. There are a variety of reasons for this change, including new occupational opportunities for women, but the largest reason appears to be that young Spaniards prefer to focus in their 20s on enjoying the freedom and fun of emerging adulthood. People in their 20s repeatedly told Douglass that marriage (and especially children) would put a damper on their ability to go out, to travel, to go skiing, to "enjoy life." This comfortable lifestyle is aided by remaining at home with their parents' care and support until marriage. Asked why they remained home well into their 20s, emerging adults in Spain would reply, "Why should we leave? We're fine here. We live in a 5-star hotel!"

Eastern Europe, after decades of oppression under communism, is rapidly headed toward the Western European model of emerging adulthood. In the Czech Republic, for example, the freedom to "work, travel, and study" during one's 20s is now highly prized. Unlike in much of the rest of Europe, low birth rates are viewed not as a crisis but as a happy manifestation of the new freedoms that Czechs gained with the fall of communism.

The lives of emerging adult "singles" are romanticized in Czech popular culture. Singles are young men and women of marriageable age who choose not to marry. They are depicted as part of a global youth culture, whose lifestyles have more in common with those of young professionals in New York and Paris than with their own parents'. But rather than resenting the enjoyments of the young, parents generally support and encourage their children to enjoy the emerging adult freedom that they never had. As elsewhere in Europe, when they finally feel ready to have children, young Czechs most frequently have one or two, and some decide to have none at all.

Europe's Beautiful Problem

If the growth and pervasiveness of emerging adulthood is a primary cause of Europe's demographic problem, what is the solution? In fact, there may not be one. Europe could let in more immigrants from countries that have much higher birth rates, but that has not worked very well so far. Clearly, the political trend at the moment in Europe is to let in fewer rather than more immigrants.

One possible note of hope is that most young Europeans hope and expect to have more children than they actually end up having. This has suggested to some observers that there may be policies that governments can develop that would encourage and allow young people to have as many children as they would like—for example, by providing free day care or more cash assistance to young parents.

I am not optimistic. (I am not an emerging adult, so I have no obligation to be optimistic.) It seems likely that the gap between how many children young people say they want and how many they actually have is mostly the result of factors that cannot be ameliorated by government policies. You get to be 28 or 30 and your soul mate does not show up on schedule. So you find someone later than you expected, and by that time you feel like you only have time to have one child after all. Or you find that you have fertility problems when you try to have your first child in your 30s. Or you have your first child and then you get divorced. Or you find a partner and you want to have two or three children but your partner does not. Or you have a first child, and you are trying to keep your career on track while also getting up frequently in the middle of the night to wipe away tears or some other bodily substance, and you decide that one child may be enough after all. States with policies strongly supporting young parents have had little success in raising their birth rates, so I doubt this will be the answer.

The other possibility is to somehow persuade emerging adults in Europe to emerge earlier, to love their leisure less, to be more willing to relinquish their self-focused fun, and to have two or three children instead of one or none. But it is difficult to see how this could be accomplished—and it may not be wise even if it were possible. The creation of emerging adulthood is something to be celebrated, not deplored. It is a great achievement of industrialized societies, a reward for hard-won affluence.

For most of human existence, life for nearly all was, if not nasty, at least brutish and short. People worked because they had to work to survive, and they had children because, well, that is what happened when you had sex now and then. People were always just one bad harvest or one mistake or a little bad luck away from deprivation and death. Now, in the space of the past century, the people of Europe and other industrialized countries have at last conquered deprivation. European societies today can afford to allow their emerging adults to search for work that is more than just a job, more than just a way of surviving, that is instead personally satisfying and an expression of their identities. Likewise, Europeans today can enjoy the ability to have as many children as they really want to have—only as many, that is, as they believe they can truly love and care for—and need not add to the numberless children throughout history who have been conceived as mere side effects of sex.

Soul mates and satisfying work will always be elusive, and Europe's demographic problem is genuine and serious. But compared to how human beings have lived in the past, and how billions of people in the rest of the world live today, these are beautiful problems to have. Think of what Europe has done in just 60 years, creating out of the rubble of World War II the most affluent, egalitarian, benevolent societies in human history, and the demographic challenge of the next century seems small in comparison. What Europe has built in the past half-century is not perfect, but it is quite wonderful, especially for emerging adults.

Jeffrey Jensen Arnett *is a research professor of psychology at Clark University and the author of* Emerging Adulthood: The Winding Road from the Late Teens Through the Twenties *(2004, Oxford University Press). During 2005 he was a Fulbright scholar at the University of Copenhagen.*

"People interested in Africa's future ought to concern themselves not just with potential conflict, but also potential political change. Youth populations are at the heart of these possibilities."

Africa's Restless Youth

Michelle D. Gavin

Scanning the horizon for insight as to what will influence the future of sub-Saharan Africa, one can immediately point to several broad baskets of important indicators. Obviously contributing to the picture are economic growth (or the lack thereof), insecure borders, increasing resource scarcity, the HIV/AIDS pandemic, and the balance of power within nations among ethnic and regional groups. However, a close look at the political engagement and political agendas of youth should also be included in the mix. Young Africans' quest for empowerment will make them significant catalysts for change.

Africa is currently in the midst of what demographers call a youth bulge. A youth bulge typically occurs when less-developed countries, with both high fertility and high mortality rates, begin to bring infant and child mortality rates down. Eventually, development gains tend to bring fertility rates down as well. But in the lag time before this occurs, a population boom of children who survive to adulthood reshapes the demographic landscape.

In Africa today, this dynamic translates into some startling figures. More than 70 percent of all Zimbabweans, for example, are now under 30; the same is true in Kenya, Uganda, Ethiopia, Liberia, and Nigeria, among other countries. Over one-third of the entire population of Zimbabwe, and over 56 percent of the adult (over 15) population, is between 15 and 29 years old. In fact, young adults (aged 15 to 29) make up 40 percent or more of the total adult population in the vast majority of sub-Saharan countries; in roughly 30 African countries, they constitute more than half of the adult population. In contrast, approximately 40 percent of the population in the United States is under 30, and young adults constitute less than 30 percent of the adult population as a whole.

Any discussion of the youth bulge in Africa risks veering into the land of breathless alarmism—*young men and street gangs and guns, oh my!*—or overcorrecting and wandering into the territory of commencement-speech clichés about how the children are indeed the future. But there is room for a closer examination of African youth that emphasizes their political role, and this should be a priority in future research. The young are more inclined to take risks, but vast youthful populations are not going to engage in violence simply for its own sake. On the other hand, violence may be a symptom of clashing political agendas.

In a region where the state has been the source of most power and economic opportunity, but governing institutions are often weak, the desires and grievances of youth are very likely to have political implications. Governments and international actors probably cannot control the degree to which youth bulges shape societies for good or for ill, but they can at least influence outcomes. Focusing too narrowly on violence and conflict rather than on underlying political tensions tends to yield a fairly sickly crop of policy prescriptions, all variations on the theme of "brace yourself." By seeking to understand youth political engagement more clearly, policy makers may be able to create conditions conducive to youth movements that do not leave a legacy of trauma and dysfunction in their wake.

Forever Young?

For the purposes of this article, I am defining youth as anyone from 15 to 29 years old. However, definitions of youth are tricky and often culturally specific. They are also subject to revision and even manipulation. Sierra Leone's National Youth Policy, for instance, targets citizens ages 15 to 35, and Sierra Leoneans sometimes use the term "youth" to describe people in their 40s—this in a country where average life expectancy for males is about 38. Last November, Zimbabwe's *Financial Gazette* questioned the youth credentials of Absolom Sikhosana, the ruling party's Youth League Secretary, suggesting that he was masquerading as a member of the 35-and-under set and that he might in fact be "past his sell-by date." In 2002, South Africa's National Youth Development Policy Framework included a youth definition of 15 to 28, but the National Youth Policy adopted in 1997 had targeted the 14-to-35 range. In any case, according to the International

Council on National Youth Policy, various South African government departments use different definitions, which rarely correspond to either of the official policies.

These variable and amorphous definitions point to an interesting phenomenon: in some African countries it is getting increasingly difficult to make the transition from youth to adulthood. Inadequate education systems combine with stratospheric unemployment rates to foreclose the possibility of securing a job that could provide financial security. This in turn makes it unfeasible to marry and start one's own family. Meanwhile, population growth has contributed to a land squeeze, and as desirable land has been divided many times over to accommodate heirs, younger siblings in particular are cut off from the prospect of inheriting workable plots.

Youths are pushed into the continent's urban centers seeking a pathway to a viable future, only to find themselves among the unemployed and alienated masses of young people already looking for the same thing. Here, they are increasingly exposed to many of the same media images of material success that bombard young people in the most developed countries—messages often crafted by marketers to explicitly target the youth demographic. The contrast between these images and their own circumstances and prospects is hard to ignore, amplifying a sense of relative deprivation.

Some young people continue their quest for opportunity by leaving their country and even the continent altogether, risking their lives by placing themselves in the hands of sophisticated and dangerous human smuggling networks that profit from the vast divide between the prospects for African and European youth.

But practical and legal constraints ensure that this pathway, like the others, is often blocked. In these situations, many of Africa's youth are caught in a Peter Pan scenario gone terribly wrong. Try as they might, they cannot seem to become adults.

Many African cultures place an extremely high premium on respect for elders. Young people are expected to know their place and to abide by the wisdom of those rich in life experience. Yet, if youth are trapped—indefinitely—in some sort of preparatory state, awaiting the time when they are accorded the respect, responsibility, and opportunity associated with being full-fledged adults in their society, it seems unreasonable to assume that they will wait patiently for a day that is nowhere in sight.

Youths have something to prove, and given opportunity, they will assert themselves. Just how violently or constructively that might happen depends on a range of factors, including the existence and nature of manipulation from older elites, the amount of political space available for civic action, and the capacity of the state and the private sector to hear and understand youth aspirations and to deliver opportunities in a relatively timely fashion.

Of course, no country's youth is monolithic. Ethnic, religious, and regional schisms can split demographic cohorts just as they can split a population at large. Also, it is often hard to discern where young women fit into the picture. This is so in part because many become mothers during this period of life, culturally moving into adulthood and a lifetime of domestic responsibility. In addition, young women's leadership and civic engagement opportunities, even within the context of youth movements, often are limited on the basis of gender alone.

Even among young men, agitation for power and respect—be it peaceful or violent—will not be the preoccupation of all youth in any setting. Nevertheless, a vocal, visible, organized segment of the youth population, particularly if it is concentrated in Africa's urban centers, can make for a movement with profound political consequences, and these political actors will be on the stage for many years to come.

Change Agents

In Africa's independence movements and struggles against colonial powers, young people played an important role in case after case. The party that governed Somalia on independence was even called the Somali Youth League. More recently, youth were pivotal in the anti-apartheid struggle in South Africa. Nelson Mandela was 26 when he and other young leaders came together to form the African National Congress Youth League in 1944; their work transformed the ANC. Later, in 1968, 22-year-old Steve Biko led the newly formed and highly influential South African Students Organization. The Soweto uprising of 1976 was grounded in secondary school students' resistance to apartheid policies, and students mobilized en masse to demand change throughout the rest of the struggle.

But today, when their demographic weight is much greater relative to older Africans' than it has been in the past, young people are most often cast in the role of a diffusely destabilizing threat, rather than as potential agents of political and social transformation. The strain of analysis that sees the youth bulge as a fundamentally threatening phenomenon often points to research that suggests a strong relationship between the likelihood of civil conflict and the existence of an urbanized youth bulge. In 2001, the US Central Intelligence Agency released a report on global demographic trends, saying of the projected youth bulges in Africa and parts of the Middle East that:

> "The failure to adequately integrate youth populations is likely to perpetuate the cycle of political instability, ethnic wars, revolutions, and anti-regime activities. . . . Increases in youth populations will aggravate problems with trade, terrorism, anti-regime activities, warfare, and crime and add to the many existing factors that already are making the region's problems increasingly difficult to surmount."

In an influential 2003 report titled *The Security Demographic,* researchers with the nongovernmental organization Population Action International found that countries experiencing a youth bulge were more than twice as likely as other countries to experience civil strife. The numbers are compelling, and so are the recent histories of devastating conflict in states like Liberia and Sierra Leone, where youth were both perpetrators and victims of appalling violence on a massive scale. It is easy to develop a generalized sense that "youth bulge" is code for marauding, angry young men.

Certainly it is not hard to understand why many African youths might have a highly developed sense of grievance. In addition to the frustrating struggle for adult status, shocking numbers of young Africans have at some point in their short lives fallen into one or more of the following unhappy categories: combatants, victims of atrocities, refugees, internally displaced persons, forced laborers, or street children.

AIDS orphans are expected to number 18 million in sub-Saharan Africa in 2010. In the worst-affected areas, their numbers are already overwhelming the capacity of extended family networks to care for them, and alternative support structures are weak or non-existent. According to UNAIDS, 6.2 million Africans 15 to 24 years old are already HIV-positive, and half of all new infections in the region occur in this age group.

The vast majority of Africa's young people have an intimate knowledge of poverty. Even elite youths are faced with a shortage of jobs in which to apply the skills they may have acquired at tremendously overcrowded, underfunded universities. Overall, according to the International Labor Organization (ILO), there are more than 17.4 million unemployed 15- to 24-year-olds in Africa, leading to a regional youth unemployment rate of 18 percent. And even the young people who do have jobs are hardly financially secure: the ILO notes that over 57 percent of African youth are working at the $1-per-day level. One can easily imagine that this cohort as a whole would be quick to blame someone or something—a governing regime or an ethnic group—for a rough past and an uncertain future.

The relationship between youth bulges and violence is important, but it speaks to just one manifestation of youth frustrations and desires. Other avenues for affecting the future include partisan political action, participation in civil society organizations, student activism, and engagement in transnational religious movements. Regardless of whether these manifold forms of expression are accompanied by violent tactics, in light of youths' demographic dominance, all of them will affect the region's future. In one way or another, young Africans are in the market for alternatives to the status quo.

This could mean significant change. In many African countries, the actors dominating the political scene have been on stage (if not in power) for quite some time. President Mwai Kibaki of Kenya is over 75 years old. President Abdoulaye Wade of Senegal is over 80. President Robert Mugabe of Zimbabwe is 83. Most existing state structures, such as party youth wings, do not actually function as entry points to party leadership. The nearly ubiquitous ministries of "youth and sports" are marginal and marginalizing institutions. They are ill-equipped to function as sustainable mechanisms for accommodating and responding to the size and potential strength of youth political activism. When voters under 29 constitute 40 percent of all registered voters, as they did in the last Liberian election, their issues and demands cry out to be mainstream priorities, not sideshows.

Tools of the Elite

Building a capacity to respond to youth demands for empowerment, rather than simply trying to keep a lid on unrest, starts with understanding the dynamics of contemporary youth's political engagement. African youth in the market for alternatives to their current situation will either generate their own vision, or adopt ones supplied by others.

Instances in which youth are manipulated and mobilized to serve an elite agenda are all too easy to come by. Military movements throughout the continent have recruited children and youth on a massive scale. Vast numbers of young Rwandans complied with the most hideous instructions during the 1994 genocide. In Zimbabwe, the ruling party established brutal camps to indoctrinate young people in the party's ideology and to train the party's youth militia.

The camps were organized in 2001 under the auspices of the National Youth Service Training Program, an initiative ostensibly aimed at improving job skills and awareness of civic responsibility. In fact, young Zimbabweans were coerced into attending training camps that taught torture techniques and exposed them to beatings and rapes in the course of molding them into new party loyalists. As the main opposition force in the country, the Movement for Democratic Change, has faltered and split, factions of it, too, have deployed young thugs to intimidate rivals. Meanwhile, the outlook for young Zimbabweans grows increasingly dim, as the national unemployment rate soars to an estimated 80 percent and the economy continues to shrink.

In 2004, disturbing reports emerged from the city of Mbuji-Mayi in the Democratic Republic of Congo. Street children and youths eager for any kind of employment had been mobilized by political elites to demonstrate in rallies and protests and to intimidate opposition figures and supporters in exchange for payment. But these young people went from being political militants for hire to becoming the victims of a massacre. Angry mobs, fed up with the crimes being committed by young people who felt empowered by their political patrons, rampaged through the city, beating and in many instances killing street children and youths.

These horrifying incidents speak to the time-honored tradition of rounding up young people and, by offering short-term opportunity (payment, license to loot, and so forth) and some proximity to power, convincing them to act as violent, visible backers of a given political power. Youth often are enlisted to support political repression and to occupy political space so as to deny it to others. From Kenya to Cameroon, the recruitment of young people to reinforce ethnic divisions, intimidate voices of dissent, and send signals about who possesses strength and power—whatever is most useful for the elites doing the recruiting—has been a regular feature of Africa's political landscape. In some cases, the formation of militant party youth wings is explicit. In other cases, direct ties to the party are less formal, perhaps protecting the party from being held accountable for disruptive youth action.

In the Driver's Seat

But instances in which youth pursue their own agendas can be found as well, and the nature of these efforts ranges from non-threatening to extremely confrontational. The sub-Saharan region is rich in dynamic, creative youth groups with a public service focus, from theater troupes dramatizing HIV/AIDS prevention techniques in Uganda to peace-building programs sustained by Tutsi and Hutu youth in Burundi. Some student groups are clearly co-opted by elites. But others, like the Kenyan University Students Organization that existed in the mid-1990s to demand democratic change, challenge the ruling class and operate as independent civil society actors.

Consider the action of some Sierra Leonean youths, including ex-combatants, in the wake of that country's devastating civil war.

These youths wanted power, but rather than focusing exclusively on personal enrichment, the Movement of Concerned Kono Youth, or MOCKY, tried to stand in for what its members perceived to be an absent or ineffective law enforcement presence. As the country's civil war wound down, MOCKY tried to fill roles one would normally associate with government—conducting patrols, monitoring mining activity, and attempting to negotiate with a multinational mining company operating in the region in an effort to secure community development commitments. Dissatisfied by what the state had to offer and longing to assert themselves in positions of leadership and authority, these youths tried to organize an alternative.

Some youth-dominated armed groups in the Niger Delta claim to have a similar agenda. Interestingly, former Nigerian dictator Sani Abacha's "two million man march" in 1998 was a turning point for youth activism. A group calling itself Youths Earnestly Ask for Abacha ostensibly organized this display of support for the regime, although the government clearly directed the entire affair. Young people from around the country were bussed to the gleaming capital city of Abuja to participate, where they saw state-of-the-art infrastructure and facilities presumably financed with Nigeria's oil wealth. The contrast between the wealth on display in Abuja and the desperately poor oil-producing communities in the Niger Delta helped to radicalize a generation.

Being used as Abacha's instruments drove the young people to develop and pursue their own agenda. No longer content to let local chiefs negotiate with the government or oil companies on behalf of communities, youth formed pressure groups and, in many cases, armed militias. Some groups remain available for hire to politicians around election time, but it is clear that these armed youth movements cannot be controlled by the state. Today, media-savvy, youth-dominated militant groups like the Movement for the Emancipation of the Niger Delta (MEND) engage in operations ranging from kidnapping foreign oil workers to hosting CNN correspondents. Their actions have consequences not only for local security, but also for international oil markets.

The Case of Ivory Coast

The distinction between youth acting as instruments and youth acting as agents is not always clear, and power between elites and youth leaders can ebb and flow. Perhaps nowhere are the lines as blurry today as they are in Ivory Coast. Once a proud island of stability and economic growth, over the past decade the country has descended into a toxic mix of civil conflict, violent xenophobia, and political stalemate—with youth as major actors throughout.

When longtime President Felix Houphouet-Boigny died in 1993, he was replaced by Henri Konan Bedie, who sought to consolidate his power by marginalizing his primary political rival, Alassane Ouattara. Bedie's method was to promote *"ivoirité"*—an ultranationalist vision of the country's identity that excluded many of the migrant workers from Burkina Faso, Mali, and Guinea who had long labored in Ivory Coast's northern agricultural fields. Not coincidentally, it also excluded Ouattara, whose main base of support was in the north, because of complicated questions about where his parents were born.

Bedie was soon overthrown in a coup, but his formula for neutralizing any political threat from Ouattara was later embraced by the current president, Laurent Gbagbo, who came to power in

2000 in a dubious election in which the two major parties' candidates were prevented from participating. A rebellion broke out in 2002, eventually splitting the country into two parts—the north and west controlled by rebels known as the *Forces Nouvelles*, and the south and east under the control of the Gbagbo government, state security forces, and their militia allies. Notably, both sides' ranks were strengthened by former combatants hardened by youth-dominated conflict in Liberia and Sierra Leone. These roving soldiers-for-hire are a new part of the regional youth landscape.

While these political machinations and the resulting conflict unfolded, global economic conditions that had been squeezing the Ivorian economy throughout the 1980s and 1990s—particularly falling prices for coffee and cocoa—began to bite ferociously. *Ivoirité* fed many elite youths' hunger for someone to blame for the scarcity of jobs, land, and opportunities. Meanwhile, northern youth became increasingly agitated about the prospect of being systematically excluded from the few opportunities available within the country. Both youth groups acted on their anxieties, led by young men who had risen to prominence as students in Ivory Coast's highly political university setting.

In fact, Guillaume Soro, the leader of the *Forces Nouvelles*, and Charles Ble Goude, leader of the pro-Gbagbo Young Patriots militia, were consecutive secretaries general of the Student Federation of Ivory Coast (FESCI) in the period from 1995 to 2001. Other militia leaders also have backgrounds as FESCI officers. FESCI was founded in the early 1990s to advocate for improved conditions at increasingly overcrowded and under-resourced university campuses; it was a movement of youth resisting the shrinking opportunities presented to them and protesting favoritism in the distribution of scholarship funds. In those early days, FESCI's dissatisfaction with government policies aligned it with the movement that advocated for multiparty politics—a movement in which the political party founded by Gbagbo (a former university lecturer himself) played an important part.

Today, the Young Patriots and allied youth militias are among the primary enforcement arms of Gbagbo's state. They can mobilize masses of youth with astonishing speed, and their activities range from the conventionally political (collecting signatures on petitions calling for the *Forces Nouvelles* to be disarmed) to the clearly repressive (prohibiting the distribution of newspapers deemed insufficiently loyal to the ruling party) to the extremely violent (brutally beating opposition supporters or simply those who appear to be of Burkinabe or Malian descent).

The International Crisis Group has documented how rural youth, some of whom had left the city after finding no employment despite having attained university degrees, have been inspired by intense state-controlled media coverage of the Young Patriots' activities to take actions that give them their own social and economic power. They set up barricades to monitor movement in and out of villages, enabling them to collect fees and attempt to reform the land tenure system according to the dictates of *ivoirité*. For their part, the *Forces Nouvelles* act as a de facto government in the territory they control, and profit from trade in cotton and arms, maintaining their own trans-boundary economic networks.

Meanwhile, FESCI lives on, allied to the Young Patriots and the Gbagbo regime. It dominates campus life by controlling access to housing, extorting money and goods, and intimidating students and professors who do not toe the ruling party line. A student organization once devoted to holding government more accountable to youth has become a zealous pro-government force. Those who have tried to form an alternative student organization have been attacked and even killed.

Thus, many youths in Ivory Coast have maneuvered through a complex political environment to establish leadership positions and sources of income for themselves in an arrangement that suits the needs and desires of the ruling political class. Others have abandoned the state structure entirely through rebellion. The country has a long history of student activism, but whereas student leaders used to graduate and move on to senior posts in government or the private sector, students more recently have constructed entirely new spaces to occupy—quite literally, in the case of the *Forces Nouvelles*.

While the ruling party and its youth enforcers are unquestionably linked, it is no longer plain that the power of the youth militias depends on patronage from the state. Political elites may be just as much hostage to the desires of the militia leaders as the other way around. Youth violence features in the case of Ivory Coast primarily as a tool married to youth leaders' own political and economic agendas. The latest peace agreement, under which Soro will serve as prime minister, offers hope of reuniting the country. But until now the country has been in a stalemate in part because the impasse benefits old and young elites in both sectors of the country, despite the fact that Ivory Coast as a whole is growing poorer.

Appeals to a Higher Power

Elsewhere in Africa, increasingly influential transnational religious movements, both Christian and Muslim, are largely fueled by African youth's enthusiastic response to alternative paths to empowerment. Faith can provide surrogate social structures and supports for those who have been through traumatic experiences and have lost other moorings. In some cases, it can also provide a form of education, which may not be available from any other source. Religious movements offer prescriptions for how to improve one's life and transform society, and in Africa today, these prescriptions have explicit political significance.

Revivalist Christian movements are thriving in much of Africa. From Malawi to Ghana, Pentecostal churches are encouraging youths to reject the "old ways" that led to poverty and despair and to embrace a faith that promises social networking opportunities, promotes links to fellow worshippers around the world, uses mass media to impressive effect, and embraces the quest for prosperity. The renewal inherent in being "born again" also speaks to the desire for an alternative to the status quo. Prominent figures within these churches can be very young themselves, exemplifying how African youth can attain respect and prominence despite the limited opportunities they may be confronted with. Moreover, unlike university-based movements, religious youth movements are accessible to non-elites.

These religious networks are not divorced from politics. A recent survey by the Pew Forum on Religion and Public Life found that 83 percent of renewalists in Kenya and 75 percent in Nigeria believe that religious groups should express views on social and political questions. And they have put this belief into action—for example, when Christians organized to help defeat a referendum on a new constitution in Kenya in 2005.

At the same time, Muslim youths may find in an Islamic revival movement a vehicle for their rejection of the status quo and desire for an alternative. In a 2005 article in the *Journal of the Royal Anthropological Institute,* Adeline Masquelier described how unemployed young men in Niger embrace a Muslim movement that condemns extravagant customs surrounding marriage (a helpful point that brings the prospect of marriage closer to their modest reach). Foreign Muslim clerics, often from Pakistan or the Middle East, have established a notable presence in the Sahel, drawing in young people to be educated in an ideology that advocates enforcing Islamic law and abandoning the secular state.

Longstanding local movements may move in new directions as young members try to effect radical change, sometimes taking cues from abroad, as with the Al Sunna Wal Jamma group of students in Nigeria that staged attacks in several northern towns in 2004. They claimed to be inspired by Afghanistan's Taliban, and apparently wished to create an Islamic state. In countries where both Christian and Muslim movements are operating, tension is inevitable. It comes as no surprise, for example, that youth have been primary players in the religiously charged communal conflicts that have plagued Nigeria in recent years.

What Next?

People interested in Africa's future ought to concern themselves not just with potential conflict, but also potential political change.

Youth populations are at the heart of these possibilities. There is a strong temptation to write off a "lost generation" in the most battle-scarred, traumatized countries, but there is no avoiding the fact that those currently holding power will not be able to wield it forever. Even those who aim to cope with vast, dissatisfied youth populations by pressing young people into the service of the ruling elite may find that, in time, their youthful foot soldiers cease to answer to their elders. Today's young people will, sooner or later, play a dominant role in society.

For policy makers, job creation clearly must be an urgent priority. A focus on educating and socializing children so that they are prepared to play a positive civic role should be another priority, particularly since so many African countries are still at an early phase of their demographic transition. In addition, by understanding youth as political actors rather than simply drivers of conflict, policy makers can aim to manage the challenge to existing orders posed by youth rather than, unrealistically, try to avoid it entirely. A viable way forward involves a thorough understanding of the various youth dynamics on the ground, and also involves a serious effort to give youth the tools, opportunities, and political space in which to pursue their interests and aspirations.

More needs to be done to shed light on how specific variables affect the capacity of youth movements to engage, reshape, and even strengthen the state. What can be done to give Africa's young people reason to believe in governing institutions or to trust that peaceful civic action can effectively address their grievances? How might a closing of the digital divide empower African youth to form new networks for change? The answers will undoubtedly vary from country to country, but the significance of the questions, and the importance of youth political engagement, will remain constant for quite some time to come.

Michelle D. Gavin *is an international affairs fellow at the Council on Foreign Relations.*

"Where the youth bulge is expanding in low-income countries . . . , the levels of frustration and conflict are certain to rise. The urgent question facing the developing world is how to improve young people's job prospects now."

For Poor Countries' Youth, Dashed Hopes Signal Danger Ahead

Richard Curtain

Young people in developing nations tend to be portrayed in the media with recurring, stereotypical images. The shy adolescent girl with headscarf and painted fingernails. The teenage mother with her malnourished child. Masked youths throwing rocks. Young men in jeans toting AK-47s. The youthful employees at a call center in India.

Snapshots like these only begin to convey the dilemmas and hardships of growing into adulthood in low-income countries. Yet the world in coming years can expect to see many more such images. The number of young people in poor nations—1.3 billion—has reached a historical high, and will continue to grow for the next two decades, peaking in 2035. In Africa, the so-called youth bulge will not peak until 2050, when 12- to 24-year-olds will reach an astonishing eight times their number in 1950.

Young people in the developing world, as a result, face very different prospects from those in affluent nations. Not only do their economic circumstances differ greatly, but the pressures they experience from their peers in the job market are poles apart. Young people in rich countries have the good fortune of seeking work in prosperous economies, and having fewer competitors for these jobs, unlike the baby boomer generation. In contrast, the burgeoning cohort of young people in poorer countries means many more of them are competing for fewer jobs in stagnant economies.

The expectations of today's young in developing countries differ from earlier generations because their identities have been shaped by the images and values of globalization. Young people, according to the Pew Global Attitudes Surveys, rate the importance of increased global trade and faster communication much more favorably than their elders in all regions in the developing world (except Latin America).

Yet those entering adulthood in low-income nations encounter a cruel and frustrating economic reality. Half of the world's active job seekers are young people, even though they make up only one in four of the working-age population. In addition, huge numbers of young people are stuck in low-paid work, locking them into extreme poverty. The resulting gap between rising expectations and limited options leads often to conflict, especially in countries with weak economies and poor governance. Without new infusions of opportunity, conditions can only grow worse as the youth bulge continues to expand.

Growing Up Global

Why are the needs of young people in developing countries important? After all, moving from childhood to adulthood is a stage in life that everyone goes through, more or less successfully. How different are the hurdles facing adolescents and twenty-somethings living outside the high income countries?

Four features of the current generation of young people in poor countries stand out. First, they are more educated and healthier than earlier generations. Three out of four 15- to 24-year-olds in developing countries are literate compared with three out of five of the 35- to 44-year-old age group. Higher education levels have raised their expectations about what they can aspire to.

Second, many more young people now live in large cities, seeking more education and testing the job market. Living in a big city can free young people from the traditional constraints of family and community and open them to new experiences and values, both good and bad.

Third, more young people through their access to education, urban living, and the media are exposed to the images and values of globalization. This process has been called "growing up global," the title of a recent report by the US National Academy of Sciences on transitions to adulthood in developing countries.

The result for many young people, according to developmental psychologist Jeffrey Jensen Arnett, is the forging of dual identities. One identity is based on a worldwide culture of practices, styles, and beliefs about freedom of choice and the rights of the individual. This helps explain, for example, why young people interviewed by Pew Global Attitudes surveys in the majority Muslim countries of Morocco, Lebanon, Jordan, Turkey, and Pakistan have a more favorable view of the United States than their elders do.

Young people's other identity is based on local traditions of family and community. In Africa, Asia, and Latin America, Pew Global Attitudes surveys show that strong majorities, regardless of age, believe that their culture is superior and are concerned about protecting their way of life. These two identities, with their divergent sets of values, often produce conflicting attitudes.

Some young people resolve this conflict by rejecting the dominant form of the global culture. They may do this by adopting a strict version of their own traditional culture. A good example is the growing tendency of young Muslim women in the United Kingdom and France to use head coverings, particularly in the face of sometimes strong reactions.

Others turn to a set of principles based on an explicit rejection of the values of the dominant globalized culture. This may involve, for example, adopting anti-consumerist lifestyles to promote a sustainable environment. Still others may espouse a highly critical view of the West based on global inequities. The *International Herald Tribune* quotes a young assistant architect from Istanbul: "It is enough to look at the economic imbalances to see why people think badly about Westerners. The United States, France, England, Germany, and many other countries have become what they are by exploiting either the natural resources or manpower of other countries. Therefore, Westerners, in this ongoing system based on exploitation, will always remain selfish and greedy."

The Expectations Gap

A fourth defining characteristic of today's younger generation in poor countries is the gap between their expectations and the opportunities open to them. Because of the pressure of their rising numbers, many are denied the chance to take advantage of their newly acquired education and health assets.

Voices of Youth, a series of consultations undertaken by the World Bank in recent years, has highlighted this problem. In Bangladesh, young people report that "the main threat in terms of finding a job is the tight labor market," the result of too many applicants for too few skilled jobs. In this situation, many young Bangladeshis see the labor market as "corrupt and nepotistic, where qualifications do not matter as much as the ability and willingness to pay a bribe or [use] kin connections. . . ."

Two common strategies for dealing with tight labor markets in the developing world are: getting as many degrees as possible or paying the necessary bribe. These experiences often have long-term damaging effects not only on individuals but also on the social cohesion of their communities.

Indeed, financial insecurity undermines young people's capacity in a variety of ways, causing them to stall on their way to attaining adult status. They find it much harder to avoid behaviors that put their health at risk; to set up a separate household, find a partner, have healthy children; and to participate politically.

Young people without education or skills have an even harder time. More than 500 million young people are estimated to live in extreme poverty. They face highly uncertain prospects, since slow economic growth is a general feature of the regions—sub-Saharan Africa, parts of South Asia, and the Middle East—where the youth share of the population is the greatest.

For many, extreme frustration leads to violence in various forms that destabilizes societies and reinforces a vicious cycle of poverty. The evidence for this is not hard to find, since most conflict-ridden poor countries have large youth populations.

Governments and international agencies have not addressed in any major way the issue of how to upgrade existing opportunities and create new avenues to help address the stymied expectations of the youth bulge. The World Bank's recently published World Development Report for 2007, entitled *Development and the Next Generation,* focuses on the need to invest in enhancing human capital. Yet the question of how the demand for these skills will be generated is not addressed.

Promoting more and better education begs the question: To what end? The image one is left with is of young men and women in their twenties, diplomas in hand, healthy and well-dressed, waiting for the call that never comes.

Youth at Risk

International agencies and governments in poor countries tend to employ one of three contrasting perspectives in considering young people—seeing them as vulnerable, as a threat, or, less commonly, as an asset.

Most governments and UN agencies regard adolescents, especially girls, as needing protection and support. The Bangladesh government, for instance, notes in its poverty reduction strategy that adolescent females have poor access to nutrition and reproductive health services and high-risk exposure to sexually transmitted diseases and HIV/AIDS. Adolescent mothers in Bangladesh account for a fifth of all births and have high rates of maternal and infant deaths. Thus, the key anti-poverty goals set for adolescent health are to reduce teenage pregnancy, provide reproductive health awareness and services to all adolescents, help prevent sexually transmitted diseases including HIV/AIDS, and reduce sexual abuse and exploitation.

Governments in postconflict situations tend to view their young people as marginalized from mainstream society, locked in a downward cycle of despair, needing protection, but usually from themselves, because of their high-risk harmful behavior. In Serbia, for example, adolescents and young adult men are seen as prone to "widespread risky lifestyles" that involve smoking, alcoholism, drug addiction, and sexual behavior.

In Sierra Leone, a decade-long civil conflict has badly affected the youth population, many of whom are now, according to a government report, "disabled, school dropouts, unemployed, commercial sex workers, drug addicts, diamond diggers, HIV/AIDS infected, sexually/physically abused young boys and girls, pregnant girls, teenage mothers, and . . . homeless." In terms of exposure to HIV/AIDS, youth and adolescents in Sierra Leone are defined as a high-risk group in the same category as commercial sex workers, uniformed personnel, migrant populations, and truck or taxi drivers.

Many of the measures concerning young people in the UN's Millennium Development Goals (MDGs) refer to these vulnerabilities. These measures are the extent of illiteracy, gender balance in formal education, HIV prevalence among young pregnant women, and young people's lack of "comprehensive and correct knowledge" of HIV/AIDS.

According to official estimates, illiteracy affects one in four young people aged 15 to 24 years in low-income countries (defined as $875 or less annual gross national income per head). However, this is certainly an underestimation of actual illiteracy levels, since many governments rely on self-reported answers. National surveys that ask respondents to read a simple sentence show higher rates of illiteracy.

The Millennium Development Goal of achieving gender balance in secondary and tertiary education has a long way to go. In South Asia, only one in two girls attends secondary school; the proportion in sub-Saharan Africa is an even smaller three in ten. In developing regions as a whole, 80 females for every 100 males are enrolled in tertiary education. Sub-Saharan Africa has the widest gender gap in tertiary enrollment (68 females to 100 males), followed by South Asia (71 females to 100 males).

The adolescent fertility rate, although not one of the MDG targets, is an important poverty indicator because it affects several Millennium Development Goals. Reducing the number of adolescent mothers would improve disproportionately the overall level of maternal health because teenage mothers, especially those who are poor, have a much higher risk of major complications from childbirth. Mothers aged 19 years and below account for nearly one in five births in the least developed countries.

Another measure of vulnerability is exposure to HIV/AIDS. Young women in sub-Saharan Africa are more prone than men to become infected with HIV/ AIDS and at an earlier age. The UN agency dealing with AIDS reports that women aged 15 to 24 years are, depending on their country, between two and six times more likely to be HIV-positive than men of a similar age. This reflects the unequal gender relations, including among youth, in most societies.

Lack of access to decent paid work is another important measure of vulnerability. However, measuring unemployment in developing countries is notoriously unreliable. Defining the unemployed as only those actively seeking work overlooks the fact that the poor cannot afford to keep looking for work. The international definition of "employed" is also too narrow. It includes work for as little as an hour a week, thus hiding the underemployed who want full-time productive jobs. The "employed" category also includes "unpaid family workers," many of whom would welcome paid work if it were available.

The International Labor Organization has recently estimated that one in five employed young people worldwide is a member of the working poor, living on $1 or less a day. In sub-Saharan Africa, the situation is especially bad: close to six out of ten young people have employment but are still living on $1 or less a day. In South Asia, four out of ten young people are working but remain in extreme poverty.

These measurement limitations mean that unemployment rates affecting young people in developing countries grossly underestimate the size of the problem. Even so, among 15- to 24-year-olds, one in three was recorded as unemployed last year in North Africa, and one in four in western Asia. In this same age group, according to another study, one in three is not currently employed or in school in Central and Eastern Europe; the same is true of one in four in sub-Saharan Africa and one in five in Central and South America.

The Conflict Connection

While young people in the developing world are seen as vulnerable, they also are often regarded as threatening. In particular, the threat to civil order posed by young men concerns many poor countries. In Latin America, youth-initiated violence and crime are common. In Moldova, the government sees the underlying cause of youth violence as young people's exclusion from the mainstream of economic life. In Kenya, officials acknowledge that young people often resort to crime, street begging, and drugs because of limited options in a depressed economy. Nigeria has seen youth violence rise in schools as well as in the wider society. Youth violence is also a major concern in the post-conflict countries of Bosnia, Nepal, Sierra Leone, Uganda, and East Timor.

Evidence of young people's links with conflict is strong. Young men represent the largest group of both victims and perpetrators of urban violence. The cities with the highest youth homicide rates are in Latin America, the United States, and the transition economies of Eastern Europe and the former Soviet Union.

Youthful populations have also been linked historically with political violence. The presence of a youth bulge in a country, in combination with other economic and social conditions, is a key factor increasing the risk of civil conflict. According to Jack Goldstone, this demographic pressure helped produce the English and French Revolutions of the seventeenth and eighteenth centuries. The same demographic pressure applies in many developing countries today.

The relevant measure is the youth share (variously defined as 12 to 24 years, 15 to 24 years, or 15 to 29 years) of the adult population (aged 15 years and above). A Norwegian researcher, Henrik Urdal, has shown that countries have a high propensity for internal armed conflict, terrorism, and rioting if they have poorly performing economies, weak governance, and a large youth share of the adult population.

It is no surprise to learn that countries with high youth bulges are mostly in sub-Saharan Africa and the Middle East (Syria, Yemen, Iran, and Jordan). The potential for conflict at subregional levels within heavily populated countries, such as India and Indonesia, can also be identified this way. A new study by Urdal of 27 states in India between 1956 and 2002 shows that the likelihood of armed conflict, political violence events, and Hindu-Muslim rioting increases with the presence of a youth bulge. This applies especially in states that also have large male surpluses and high levels of urban inequality.

Do poor countries with large youth bulges recognize the problem? Some sub-Saharan countries, such as Burkina Faso, Lesotho, and Sierra Leone, do give a prominent place in their poverty reduction strategies to the needs of young people. Other countries, such as Kenya, Tanzania, Bangladesh, and Nicaragua, only give minor attention to youth issues. And the governments of Pakistan, Nigeria, Uganda, and Nepal—despite their huge youth populations—give no recognition at all to the needs of young people in their national poverty reduction strategies.

Measures of Worth

Less commonly, governments in low-income countries view youth in positive terms, not merely as vulnerable or threatening but as assets to be invested in and supported. This focus encourages the provision of more resources to provide all young people with a basic level of education and to enhance their life skills with relevant occupational or entrepreneurial training. Other policies include providing better access to credit and opportunities to study abroad to learn best practices.

Asset-based measures of young people are much less common than measures of their vulnerabilities. One such measure is completed years of education. Reliable data on this are hard to find, but in many countries relatively small numbers of youth progress from primary to secondary school. The reasons are poor preparation, lack of interest, and high costs.

Years of completed education, however, are now increasingly seen as an inadequate measure as new information about learning achievement becomes available. International student assessment surveys show that the level of basic skills among 15-year-old students in Indonesia, Thailand, Tunisia, Brazil, Turkey, Uruguay, and Mexico is about 20 percent lower than the scores of students in high-income countries. The poorest students in these countries have even lower scores. Nor can it be assumed that completion of primary school confers literacy. Many young people in poor countries with several years of primary school education are functionally illiterate.

The measure most associated with the "young people as asset" perspective is the ratio of the working population to the dependent age population (children to 15 years and adults 65 years and older). This calculation highlights the window of opportunity available to governments to reap the benefits of investing in the enhancement of the skills of the young working population.

They had better act quickly. Of the world's inhabitants in extreme poverty—living on less than $1 per day—one in five is aged 15 to 24 years. Where the youth bulge is expanding in low-income countries that are burdened with poor governance and weak economies, the levels of frustration and conflict are certain to rise. The urgent question facing the developing world is how to improve young people's job prospects now.

Working Assets

There are a number of ways, in fact. Some involve scaling up existing efforts, others adopting new approaches. In particular, encouraging youth entrepreneurship has been widely touted, but little action has been taken. This may change with Kenya's recent decision to set up a "youth employment fund" to promote entrepreneurship, with an endowment of $14 million. Other governments in Africa and elsewhere may follow suit if the endeavor proves successful.

Because of their skills, available time, and interests, young people have a comparative advantage in entrepreneurial activities based on computers and use of the Internet. Many pilot projects have been tried in developing countries, but few have been evaluated critically to find out which should be scaled up. Since small business opportunities in weak economies are limited, access to high-income markets, through the Internet, offers much better prospects. Also needed is on-the-ground support from rich countries through peer networks based on youth associations. Diaspora networks could be tapped as potential markets.

Improved access to microcredit for young people is essential. The success of microcredit comes from showing that the poor are "bankable," but the main beneficiaries have been stable groups of older married women. Young unmarrieds are viewed as poor credit risks. Thus, the young self-employed need first to prove the viability of their enterprise by persuading family and friends to support them, at least initially. This will enable them to develop a credit profile based on their achievements.

Proposed new investments in transportation infrastructure in Africa will be a major job generator. For young people to benefit, construction initiatives should include targets for employing youth age groups, provided they meet basic competency standards set by employers. Construction firms should also be asked to train young people on the job, through the use of mentors. Governments will need to fund front-end skills training separately, based on national skill standards, to ensure that economy-wide gains are achieved.

Overseas temporary work is another option for both semi-skilled and skilled young people. Many small countries with populations of less than 2 million simply lack the opportunities for young people with talent. They do not have the critical population threshold needed to support a diversified economy. The option of working overseas is a major source of income for many low-income countries. Money sent back home usually goes directly to the poorest households.

Several sending and receiving countries have temporary labor migration programs. Jamaica has a bilateral hospitality worker program with the United States, which arranges the temporary migration of Jamaicans to work in the American hospitality industry, primarily as cooks and maids. Canada's Seasonal Agricultural Workers Program, established in 1974, allows Mexican migrants to work on Canadian farms for up to eight months a year. Selection for the program is restricted to family heads with little formal education and low income. The workers have been able to save to send their children to school, invest in their farms, and improve their homes.

Overseas temporary skilled work can provide unexpected wider benefits for poor economies in the form of a major incentive for more young people to lift their education and skill levels. Universities will be under pressure from their students to increase the quality and relevance of their education to match the standards of the destination countries. The result is a larger domestic skills pool of higher quality.

Governments need to play their part too in enhancing the capacities of their young people. One option, tried in only a few countries, is to set up a domestic Peace Corps–like national service for young people to undertake civic service work through projects such as literacy training and malaria eradication. In Nigeria, university graduates can provide civic service in a rural location such as a high school, community health center, or agricultural extension. Another option for national service in developing countries would help those with basic literacy skills to run small maintenance businesses to meet the demand for rural services in water, sanitation, and electricity. A third strategy would use the skills of educated young people to engage with their illiterate peers by combining literacy training with other activities such as environmental conservation or health promotion.

Potential for Change

The situation facing young people in the developing world deserves much more attention than it has received. Their vulnerability in terms of low incomes, illiteracy, and poor education outcomes has received little focus in the poverty reduction strategies of governments and international agencies. The effects of large youth cohorts on developing countries have been largely ignored by governments and others, apart from those concerned with identifying preconditions for peace and security.

The view of young people as critical assets for lifting economies and societies out of poverty offers the most potential for change, yet it has gained the least attention. Governments, international agencies, and donors could harness far better the capacities of young people. To do this effectively, they need to encourage and support young entrepreneurs, help them find ways to take advantage of technology and globalization to access high income markets, and promote antipoverty efforts that mobilize young people's collective energies. Above all, governments need to engage directly and constructively with young people themselves. This requires actively including them in the political process and meaningfully responding to their needs and aspirations.

Richard Curtain *is a public policy consultant based in Melbourne, Australia, who has worked with UNICEF and the UN Population Fund.*

"Membership in a clandestine terrorist cell; online linkages with glamorous, dangerous individuals; the opportunity to belong to a feared and seemingly heroic movement complete with martyrs—all of this is inherently appealing to young people."

Toy Soldiers: The Youth Factor in the War on Terror

Cheryl Benard

"About the time of Easter . . . , many thousands of boys, ranging in age from six years to full maturity, left the plows or carts which they were driving, the flocks which they were pasturing, and anything else which they were doing . . . [and] put up banners and began to journey to Jerusalem. . . . They [said] that they were equal to the Divine will in this matter and that, whatever God might wish to do with them, they would accept it willingly and with humble spirit. Some were turned back at Metz, others at Piacenza, and others even at Rome. Still others got to Marseilles, but whether they crossed to the Holy Land or what their end was is uncertain. One thing is sure: that of the many thousands who rose up, only very few returned."

—*From a description of the so-called Children's Crusade in* Chronica Regiae Coloniensis Continuatio prima, *translated by James Brundage*

Much has been made of an ominous demographic reality prevalent in the Middle East. Although the exact number varies from country to country, any speaker who mentions the proportion of the population below age 20, or below age 16, can count on receiving gasps of surprise from Western audiences. Fifty percent of the population below age 19! Sixty-five percent below age 25! And no functioning economy to absorb them. It is clear even to a layperson that this spells trouble.

Experts will point out that it could also spell prosperity—in theory. In theory, a young population has the potential to be productive and to bless its society with a low dependency ratio: that is, with a larger segment of productive workers supporting a smaller segment of the elderly, the very young, the incapacitated, and otherwise nonproductive individuals who must count on tapping into the income of others. In reality, though, cultural, political, and economic factors can—and throughout much of the Islamic world do—stand in the way of productivity and prosperity. The youth overhang, instead of constituting a motor for growth, becomes what Isobel Coleman of the Council on Foreign Relations has called a potential "youthquake" and a "massive demographic tsunami."

Many young people in the Middle East, especially the famously more volatile young males, are deprived of sensible activities, bereft of real hope for a happy and independent future, unschooled in practical modes of thinking, and sexually frustrated in their strict and puritanical societies. Many are hammered with the rousing appeals of radical preachers and ideologues. Others are simply bored and purposeless. Clearly this is not a promising recipe for stable social advancement.

All of these social conditions and their implications in the region are being discussed and fretted over, and with good cause. But another variable in the situation has received less attention: the underlying mindset and mental development of young adults generally. I would argue that, beneath many of the conflicts tearing at the Middle East today, including the "war on terror," the Palestinian intifada against Israel, and the insurgency in Iraq—as indeed underneath probably most instances of major violence throughout history—there lies an unspoken, disturbing social contract in which older people pursue agendas by deploying the volatile weapon of mentally not-yet-mature younger men.

The Immature Brain

While this issue has important ethical dimensions, the question is raised more neutrally by recent neurological and developmental findings that in turn are the product of improved medical technology. Increasingly sophisticated Magnetic Resonance Imaging (MRI) of brains, in combination with research in experimental psychology, indicates that maturation may take place more gradually and conclude later than formerly presumed. A number of studies suggest that mental and behavioral development continues to be in considerable flux until somewhere between the ages of 22 and 24; that before this time, young people and particularly young men are inclined to show particular responses, behaviors, and mindsets; and that these are of high relevance to their own personal safety and well-being and to those of others around them.

The findings can be summed up as follows: young men are strongly inclined to seek out situations of risk, excitement, and danger; and they also are likely to make fallacious judgments about their own abilities, overestimating their capacities and underestimating objective obstacles and dangers. In a variety of important interactive contexts, as a result, their reactions predictably veer toward the impulsive taking of unwise risks. All of this affects their ability not so much to understand, but to process and "believe in" the potential for negative outcomes and even catastrophic consequences of their decisions.

Not much of this, of course, really comes as a surprise. That young people are impulsive and that young men like to test themselves in situations of high risk is well known. Recent research, however, provides a much more specific window into the mechanics of youthful responses and decisions, as well as the situations that represent a particular risk for reactions that can be harmful to the individual or to others. It also reveals the inherence of some of these behaviors, which are not individual failings or errors but flow from a natural developmental process to which all individuals are subject—and which others might exploit.

The first conclusion that suggests itself from current research in neurological development is that adolescence and young adulthood conclude later than formerly assumed. Brain development is of course an ongoing process. Adolescence, however, is a time of particularly high change. Longitudinal studies following changes in the prefrontal cortex indicate that the changes do not wind down until age 22 or even later. The prefrontal cortex is jovially referred to by experts in this field as the "area of sober second thought." This is the part of the mind that carefully considers the consequences of a decision, weighs the pros and cons, reflects, and, depending on the evidence, may come to reconsider. In the absence of a fully developed prefrontal cortex, an individual will be more inclined to follow through on a spontaneous, impulsive decision.

In a 2004 study titled "Adolescent Brain Development and Drug Abuse," Ken Winters of the University of Minnesota noted that three brain structures that undergo maturation during youth—the nucleus accumbens, amygdale, and prefrontal cortex—have important implications for understanding adolescent behavior. "An immature nucleus accumbens is believed to result in preferences for activities that require low effort yet produce high excitement. . . . The amygdale is the structure responsible for integrating emotional reactions to pleasurable and aversive experiences. It is believed that a developing amygdale contributes to two behavioral effects: the tendency for adolescents to react explosively to situations rather than with more controlled responses, and the propensity for youth to misread neutral or inquisitive facial expressions of others as a sign of anger. And one of the last areas to mature is the prefrontal cortex . . . responsible for the complex processing of information, ranging from making judgments to controlling impulses, foreseeing consequences, and setting goals and plans. An immature prefrontal cortex is thought to be the neurobiological explanation for why teenagers show poor judgment and too often act before they think."

Recent MRI and brain mapping research has also focused on the cerebellum, a part of the brain formerly thought to relate primarily to physical movement, but now found to coordinate a variety of cognitive processes and to enable individuals to "navigate" social life. As Jay Giedd of the National Institute of Mental Health, among others, has pointed out, this portion of the brain is not fully developed until well into the early twenties.

Besides magnetic resonance imaging, a second strand of research employs experiments to measure the responses and the decision making of individuals in relation to an assortment of variables, among them, age and gender. These include tests that place an individual in simulated decision-making scenarios, such as a driving situation in which he or she must make a split-second decision on whether or not to proceed through an intersection; tests that require the individual to override a physical reflex, for example by deliberately not looking in the direction of a suddenly bright light; gambling tasks that measure risk aversion; and many more. Young men perform very poorly on all of these tasks.

Thrill Seekers

In turn, outcomes suggested by the findings of both of these research methods are reflected in broader social data. Changes that begin with adolescence and conclude at the end of young adulthood incline young people, and young men in particular, to seek excitement, to misjudge situations, and to dismiss danger. These inclinations are clearly readable in morbidity rates, which increase by a dramatic 200 to 300 percent between childhood and full adulthood.

Roadside accidents, for example, are one arena in which this plays itself out. In a 2005 study commissioned by the Allstate Foundation, accident fatalities and car-related injuries to young drivers were studied in collaboration with Temple University, which brought neuropsychiatric and experimental findings to bear in an analysis of accident causation. The study noted that "key parts of the brain's decision-making circuitry do not fully develop until the mid-20s. So, in actual driving situations, teens may weigh the consequences of unsafe driving quite differently than adults do. This, combined with the increased appetite for novelty and sensation that most teens experience at the onset of puberty, makes teens more disposed to risk-taking behind the wheel—often with deadly results."

Males below the age of 24 have nearly three times as many accidents as their older counterparts; their accidents are significantly more likely to be fatal; and accident analysis reveals that the young men are almost always at fault. This is not attributable, as some might suppose, to a lack of experience or technical skill. Rather, the problem lies in the propensity of young men to take risks, to misjudge or ignore danger, and to make erroneous split-second decisions on the basis of factually unwarranted optimism and overconfidence. Young people are also substantially more likely to make the decision to drive while under the influence of alcohol or drugs.

The Allstate study found that conventional drivers' education programs are not effective in countering these dangerous youthful inclinations. They can enhance skill levels and convey information, including warnings about dangers and advice about safer decisions, but they do not affect the underlying impulses and motivators. Interestingly, the expedient of placing a female passenger in the vehicle with the young male driver effects more improvement in safe driving than a lecture or a class. Having him joined by another young male, on the other hand, will increase the likelihood of reckless driving.

Another example of how young adulthood differs from both childhood and full adulthood can be found in recent research on Post Traumatic Stress Disorder—in particular, a study published in the October 2006 issue of the *American Journal of Psychiatry.* Research conducted at Walter Reed Army Medical Hospital on veterans of combat in Afghanistan and Iraq found that soldiers below age 25 are 3.4 times more likely to experience Post Traumatic Stress Disorder than older soldiers. This is in accordance with other research showing that adolescence and young adulthood are a time of particular vulnerability to stress, and an age at which grief and loss are felt with enhanced severity.

A few caveats are in order before speculating on the political significance of these insights into young people's mentality. First, this research is fairly young and we may come, at some future point, to challenge or even reverse its findings. Second, the determinism of responses and behaviors varies. The mere fact that inclinations or reflexes push an individual in a certain direction does not mean that he or she is unable to override them; it just means that this may be more difficult.

Finally, the point being made by the research is that maturation is a process. The findings do not mean that individuals are irresponsible and volatile until, at some arbitrary point, be it 18 or 21 or 22 or 24, they suddenly emerge as mature and sober adults. Maturation unfolds at different rates and to different degrees; it seems reasonable to presume, though this has not yet been studied, that much will also depend on the surrounding societal circumstances, on education, and on other variables affecting the life circumstances and influences operating on the individual young adult.

It remains nonetheless a telling fact that, within the Middle East and Muslim communities worldwide, young males constitute the most numerous participants in violent behavior and pose the greatest security threat to Western societies. Indeed, Western European security agencies report that radicalization among European Muslim minority communities is manifesting itself at ever-younger ages, with 14 and 15 now the typical age at which young people are drawn into extremism. (The most effective recruiting tool today is the Internet.)

It is not difficult to see that propensities inherent in this age group, and effective until age 24 or so, make this subpopulation an ideal audience for radical recruitment. Membership in a clandestine terrorist cell; online linkages with glamorous, dangerous individuals; the opportunity to belong to a feared and seemingly heroic movement complete with martyrs—all of this is inherently appealing to young people. And membership comes with flaming speeches, weapons, face-masks, and all the accoutrements of a forbidden armed struggle. Better-adjusted male teenagers satisfy their craving for excitement with video games; those who belong to a disaffected minority may be drawn, at least in some instances, to the real thing.

How Real is Real?

After all, when you are an adolescent, how real is real? The question cannot yet be scientifically measured, but we can glimpse an answer in some of the Muslim suicide bomber videos circulating on the Internet. Do not look, for the moment, at the chanting group of celebrants surrounding the prospective bomber. Ignore the splendid, resolute text he is reading from his notes. Look instead at his face, and take note of the momentary expression of surprise, even shock. Did this young man, when he signed up to become a suicide bomber, truly understand that this moment would come, that it would feel like this, that it would be real and irreversible? His expression suggests otherwise, but there is no turning back, not with the video camera rolling and his cheering comrades ready to pack him into the truck—where in many cases, to strengthen his resolve, he will be handcuffed to the steering wheel.

Similarly, the teenagers who place improvised explosive devices (IEDs) on the streets of Baghdad may not have thought very far beyond the money, or the approbation of their clique, with which this act is rewarded. US intelligence officers report seeing children, including a 14-year-old girl, placing roadside IEDs. Iraqi officials report capturing near the Syrian border a 10-year-old boy who had "come to wage jihad."

This is not to dismiss the more elaborate, complex approaches that are being put forward to explain and respond to the threat of Islamist radicalism, global terrorism, and the insurgency in Iraq. Certainly, political and ideological and cultural and ethnic and economic and perhaps religious reasons play a part. But with all of that, it would be a mistake to forget that most of the minds involved are very young and acting on impulses and a logic that any proposed solutions should take into account.

It is necessary to mention, as well, that the same is true on the other side of this conflict. If America's adversaries in Iraq, for example, are primarily young, then so are the soldiers that the United States is sending forward to confront them. There is some difficulty in criticizing Islamist recruitment videos aimed at teenage viewers, when the online game "America's Army" similarly seeks to rope in 14-year-olds for subsequent service. This multiplayer interactive online game is a recruiting tool created by the US military. It is popular because of its excellent graphics and because it is free. Research conducted by the US military shows that the game is instrumental in the decision of numerous young people to join the actual armed services.

The point here obviously is not to equate the goal of these two "recruiting agencies." The point is that 14-year-old males are largely vulnerable to the promise of thrills and danger and largely oblivious to risk, and that—if the research cited above is correct—they will not have changed enough by 17 or 18 years of age to assure that their decision to join a war and risk death and dismemberment has been judicious, thoughtful, and taken in full understanding of what it can entail. Research on young people's brain development also implies that militaries ought, at a minimum, to consider some of the revealed inclinations and predispositions of young adults in their training and deployment of younger soldiers. Thus, a propensity to interpret facial expressions as reflecting hostility can clearly be detrimental in interactions with civilian populations, for example in house searches.

More generally, developmental research raises provocative questions for a US intervention in Iraq in which the largest proportion of casualties is borne by troops aged 21 and below. Do optimistic risk assessments and split-second decisions in favor of the more dangerous path play a role? Does the United States really have a "volunteer army" if very young adults have an impaired ability to judge the consequences of their decisions? And perhaps most intriguingly of all: What would the "war on terror" look like if neither side could deploy large numbers of young men with high affect, operating on hair-trigger responses, and low on "sober second thought"?

Cheryl Benard *is a senior political scientist with the RAND Corporation and director of RAND's Initiative on Middle East Youth. She is the author of* Civil Democratic Islam *(Rand, 2004).*

"Repressive measures that have targeted youth gangs and criminalized the younger generation threaten the progress of both human rights and democracy."

Youth, Violence, and Democracy

Paulo Sérgio Pinheiro

The French sociologist Pierre Bourdieu once suggested that everyday violence is a solvent of human integrity. The levels of violence that are found today in almost every Latin American country constitute a true demonstration of this insight, testifying to the devastating effects of everyday brutality. And no one is more involved in this violence, both as perpetrators and victims, than the region's impoverished youth.

Some two decades after the fall of many dictatorships in Latin America—a phenomenon that raised so many hopes and allowed those of us who fought to establish democracy to dream—there is a bitter sense in the air. Campaigns for harsh, repressive measures against the poor and the young, disguised as justified wars against crime, find consistent and wide support among the local population. In this context, those who support human rights are confronted with considerable skepticism, if not threats and rejection, from many sectors of society.

It is not very difficult to understand why. Despite improvements in the juridical sphere, and despite the relatively calm and fair electoral processes introduced by democratization, an *un-rule of law* continues to be a daily reality for millions of people across Latin America. Economic inequality has also increased, and the already fragile welfare state has shrunk to a minimum—deepening a widespread sense of insecurity. Perhaps most disturbingly, the levels of violence in Latin America are among the highest in the world, so much so that in some cases they surpass the mayhem in armed-conflict areas.

The situation faced by children and youth is especially critical. Data on homicides drawn from a World Health Organization study show that Latin American youth are the group most targeted for violence in the world. About 29 percent of homicides in Latin America are inflicted on children and youth from 10 to 19 years of age. Available figures indicate that homicide is the second-leading cause of death for this age group in 10 of the 21 countries of the region that have populations of over 1 million inhabitants. Youth homicide rates can be up to three times higher than national homicide rates. In Venezuela, for example, 95 percent of homicide victims are male and 54 percent of them are younger than 25.

Media coverage, as well as the issues that feature in the political agenda of Latin American leaders, indicates that the involvement of youth in criminal activities and gangs is a particular preoccupation among the nations of the region. An assessment of the reasons for this situation, and of the government responses that have been implemented, suggests that youth violence and the reactions to it are directly linked to the weakness of democratization in Latin America.

The Gangs of Central America

One place where youth violence has provoked great public insecurity is Central America, where youth gangs known as *maras* or *pandillas* have surged in the past decade. Concerns about maras, aired dramatically during election campaigns, have led local governments to elaborate ultra-tough anti-gang strategies that have attracted international attention, especially from human rights organizations. The phenomenon of maras, in fact, sheds an important light on the problem of youth violence in Latin America, in particular as organized and armed gangs expand, and allows us to reflect on the common problems found in state responses to these groups.

In my capacity as an Independent Expert appointed by the UN Secretary General to conduct a study of violence against children, I led a mission a year ago to El Salvador, Guatemala, and Honduras to gather information on the situation of the maras and the anti-maras plans. Before our mission, I was of course aware of violence in that region. But it is one thing to have information, to read reports, to know the statistics. It is another to meet with all the players in the tragedy—the *mareros* (gang members), their families, the police, the human rights activists, the judges, and the authorities—including then-President Ricardo Maduro of Honduras, one of the initiators of the so-called *mano dura* (hard hand) approach to youth violence.

After seeing in those countries—as well as in my own country, Brazil—the degrading and devastating effects of violence inflicted against stigmatized populations, it is difficult to talk about the young and the poor and the oppressed in an accurate and realistic way, and without appearing either to cast them simply as perpetrators of crime or to exalt them for their resistance and resilience. As Bourdieu, among other scholars, has observed, "the inclination to violence is engendered by early and constant exposure to violence." This is one of the most tragic effects of the condition of poor communities throughout Latin America and the Caribbean.

The maras, like other youth gangs, are formed through the common experiences of their members and, as such, constitute communities. They also change their behavior and objectives in accordance with the context in which they exist. The emergence of the first maras occurred perhaps more than two decades ago, but the transformation of these groups into a key public security concern is a more recent development.

The maras are formed mostly by young people between 16 and 25 years of age. They establish and enforce codes of loyalty and conduct. The majority of mara members display external symbols such as tattoos, exhibit specific body language, and wear distinctive clothing, thereby delineating clear territories of control and rivalry among different gangs. In many cases, mara members get involved in armed violence. The number of gang members and the real impact of the gangs on public security are motifs of many creative—and absolutely unreliable—governmental statistics. Indeed, in some instances during my mission to Central America, the figures quoted to us by different sources in the same ministry varied by 200 percent.

I am aware that the definition of gang membership has plagued researchers of youth violence since they began to study the phenomenon. I am also aware that the very concept of the gang is frequently convenient for those who wish to use the term in a discriminatory way. But one of the defining features that has separated benign organizations from traditional street gangs is involvement in criminal activity, often a reflection of the shared experience of the members.

When You're a Marero

Our discussions with adolescents during our visits in Central America clearly demonstrated that some factors are common to the life histories of mara members, pointing to root causes for their engagement in these sorts of groups. The majority of gang members came from the poorest sectors of the population and had no access to a proper education, having been abandoned or expelled from local schools.

The Public Opinion Institute of Central American University in El Salvador conducted a survey of 1,025 gang members in the San Salvador metropolitan area and found that 75 percent were unemployed. Among those employed, only half held stable jobs. And only 33 percent of those surveyed had finished high school. About 76 percent had dropped out of school.

Many of the adolescents we interviewed during the UN mission came from disrupted families, with some having faced domestic violence within their homes. Many had absolutely no expectations of finding any sort of employment. The majority of mareros were involved with petty crime around the communities that they dominated. They also had severe conflicts with gang rivals.

One tragic reality in Latin America is that violence is frequently directed by the dispossessed against their companions in misfortune. Youth gangs often use violence to meet their members' economic and social needs, further adding to already high levels of violence in their communities. For example, in my own country, the majority of homicides in São Paulo and Rio de Janeiro are committed among the working class. Very few of my white and elite compatriots are murdered and even fewer are the object of state violence.

This is no accident. The everyday violence exerted in families, factories, streets, offices, police stations, and prisons—including the violence committed by and against young people—is in the last analysis an effect of the inherent violence of economic structures, income concentration, and structural racism. This is manifested sooner or later in the form of crime and delinquency, drug addiction, alcoholism, and a whole host of minor and major everyday acts of violence—including gang violence.

Economic policies that aggravate the situation of the majority of families and their children are assiduously implemented by governments, including those described as leftist, immediately when they take power. James Vigil of the University of California at Irvine has written of the "multiple marginalities" that affect mareros. These certainly are aggravated by global processes like economic restructuring and democratic transitions after war and regional peace settlements. Frequently, during my conversations with mareros, I heard the background echo of violence as the reproduction of violent patterns internalized during civil war.

Central America's conflicts during the 1980s produced a mass migration from the region, mainly to the United States. The subsequent deportation of large groups of people back to Central America appears to have created a generation of youth who do not have clear ties either to North American communities (where most of them lived in very marginalized areas and were sometimes the victims of discrimination) or to their communities in El Salvador or Honduras. One result of these upheavals was the dismantling of local webs of family and community life, the terrain where daily interactions are sustained.

Out of these dynamics has emerged an inner-city culture—*una cultura callejera*—that seeks to replace these vanished bonds, whose absence is itself made worse by the lack of education, pervasive non- or under-employment, and a lack of social investment. In this context, the maras in a certain way represent a reconstruction of those elements that were lost and cannot be recovered. But this reconstruction constitutes a terrible burden for these young people, even as it requires enormous inventive capacities.

Across Latin America, the growth in gang membership has coincided with easy access to small arms. In a number of countries, past conflicts have facilitated the spread of small arms, identified by the World Health Organization as a key factor leading to the escalation of lethal violence in the region. In Brazil, homicides among youth have increased 77 percent in a decade, mainly because more violence has involved firearms.

The Resort to Repression

The Central American states' responses to the maras issue have had an important and negative impact and, at the same time, are revealing about Latin America's repressive tendency vis-à-vis youth violence. Public security has become a major political issue, with strident anti-maras policies serving as prominent leitmotifs in both administration policy making and election campaigns. In El Salvador and Honduras, new laws and changes in the penal code have created specific penalties for those who are considered to be mara members or are committing the crime of "illicit association."

These legal instruments have gone so far as to stipulate that the mere existence of indicia such as tattoos, certain clothes, or graffiti is sufficient for youngsters to be detained for long periods. Legal reforms in this area also have called into question recently established codes for children and adolescents, providing that mara members less than 18 years old can be tried in adult courts as adults. Many of these legal changes contradict existing national, regional, and international standards and guidelines, including prescriptions set forth by the Convention on the Rights of the Child.

The concrete results of these measures are also appalling. During our mission we heard frequent allegations of abusive and sometimes arbitrary detention of hundreds of suspected gang members, with the result that detention centers have rapidly filled and have become increasingly violent. In Honduras, two riots at such facilities between the end of 2003 and the beginning of 2004 resulted in 1,500 casualties. With violence reproduced behind bars as the gang members are imprisoned, the violence perpetrated by some maras appears to have increased. Certainly, violent rivalries between opponent gangs have grown in detention facilities, and the linkages between some potential members and their maras are enhanced.

Governments' aggressive responses to the maras reflect a sharp escalation in public rhetoric. In El Salvador, the first version of the state's anti-gang strategy was called Mano Dura, the second Super Mano Dura (heavy hand and super heavy hand). Anti-Maras Squads were created (mixing police and army—one of Latin America's favored approaches). And you would even hear references to the beginning of "mara hunting season." Some of these hunts included the president as the convoy leader. Opinions found daily in newspapers reproduce and reinforce public perceptions of the linkage between maras and the vast majority of crimes.

"Moral Panic"

These phenomena are not, of course, exclusive to Central Americans. Barry Feld of the University of Minnesota Law School has noted that "public frustration with crime, fear of the recent rise in youth violence in all continents, and the racial characteristics of violent young offenders fuel the desire 'to get tough' and provide political impetus to prosecute a larger number of youths as adults." In a 2002 essay titled "Moral Panic and Youth Violence," three Rutgers University researchers described similar scenarios within Central America and outside it, in which the media and political establishment publicized "exaggerated claims of danger posed by unconventional youths; in turn, inflammatory rhetoric was used to justify enhanced police powers and greater investment in the traditional criminal apparatus."

It is relevant to acknowledge that the "moral panic" created by the maras is not sheer paranoia (even paranoids may have real enemies). The problem of youth violence touches on bona fide social ills that democratic governance must seriously address. Unfortunately, rather than directing the public toward an informed understanding of the problem, in the case of the mano dura rhetoric and in other Latin American wars against gangs, the media and the politicians instead pander to popular fear. The result is renewed hostility toward people who are easy to identify and dislike—the "torturable" classes, as Graham Greene described them.

The fragile implementation of reforms to the juvenile justice system also exhibits daily contradictions. Despite some good efforts, the "new" never quite replaces the old in Latin America. When it comes to youth in trouble, discourses of protection, restoration, punishment, responsibility, rehabilitation, welfare, retribution, and human rights continue to exist alongside each other in a perpetually uneasy and tremendously contradictory manner. Statements clouded in layers of rhetoric regarding the best interest of the child are spoken in tandem with the practice of incarcerating youth—thereby condemning some of them to abuse, torture, and sexual assaults—for their alleged education and training. The juvenile justice system implemented in many Latin American countries (including the three most affected by maras) reproduces the same problems that you might find in the adult system. These include slow responses to cases, an extremely high number of non-processed detainees, and a chaotic situation within detention centers.

In this respect, the juvenile justice system in the region is as bad as the one designed for adults, yet it is weaker in keeping offenders detained. Therefore, it is not very surprising to see broad popular support for proposals directed at reducing the age of criminal responsibility or creating exceptions that would allow children to be tried as adults, as proposed in the mano dura plans.

Forces of Resistance

It may help to understand the general situation in Latin America today, and especially the way democracy is perceived, if we consider the tragic linkage between limited democratization and the rise of youth violence. Latin America has undergone a democratization process with important achievements, restricted mostly to the institutional level. A recent report by the United Nations Development Program (UNDP) notes that, at present, established electoral mechanisms exist throughout Latin America, and the region is moving toward juridical and institutional adaptation to the principal international human rights standards.

At the same time, this progress has not been replicated in the population's social and economic situation. The entire region is marked by severe inequality. That is clearly the case of the three countries I visited. According to the UNDP, 79 percent of the Honduran population lives in poverty. In El Salvador, the underground market employs an estimated 42 percent of the workforce. In Guatemala, access to education is very difficult for the rural population—only 24 percent of schools are in the rural areas, where 60 percent of the country's school-age population is concentrated.

And despite the advances of democracy, it must be noted that legal rights and the rule of law continue to be elusive—particularly for the majority of poor Latin American young people. The region continues to struggle with seemingly intractable problems in criminal justice: abusive use of lethal force by police forces, extra-judicial killings , lynching, torture, abominable prison conditions, and persistent corruption. These phenomena abide despite numerous attempts to eradicate them by legislative reforms and institution building.

Most Latin American countries have ratified core human rights conventions and comply with the international and regional human rights regimes. They have designed special rights policies and introduced national human rights institutions, including police ombudsman offices. They have encouraged the organization of civil society, which has expanded extraordinarily. And yet, although at first such policies and measures flourish, within a few years each seems to lose efficacy and credibility.

Beatriz Affonso of the Center for Justice and International Law in Brazil has studied, for example, the efficiency of legislation that removed from the military police the privilege of trial by military courts in cases of homicide against civilians in São Paulo. Her research shows that impunity continues to reign because public prosecutors (with the Ministério Público) do not pressure the police forces to carry out proper investigations and in fact seem to be in collusion with the police to drop charges. In general, the forces within the state apparatus and in the political arena that resist change seem to prevail.

This trend is the opposite of what was forecast by democratic transition theories. It was expected that, as democratic political systems developed, there would be a clear reduction in human rights violations. Among human rights violations, none is more pervasive in Latin America than the violence against children and young people perpetrated or condoned by democratic governments.

This unfortunate dynamic is helping to create a perverse linkage between the adoption of modern international human rights standards and official reactions to youth violence. In Central America and throughout Latin America, there is a spreading incapacity or unwillingness on the part of governments to guarantee the right to life of their populations. On the contrary, under the pretext of carrying out wars on crime, governments are in reality undermining the rule of law and weakening their societies' support for the concept of democracy.

The Mantra of Prevention

How can we prevent conventional youth and teen groups from becoming violent without resorting to repressive measures and public rhetoric that are counterproductive and undermine democracy? How can we make violent communities safer and more stable? How can we break the cycle of violence and reintegrate back into society the young people who have decided to engage in illicit activities? What are the root causes that need to be urgently addressed to produce sustainable gains?

These are not easy questions. As everyone is aware, there are no easy and fast solutions. There are no prêt-à-porter plans that can be developed and replicated everywhere without regard for local circumstances. We are working with problems that have deep connections with communities and their recent histories.

Still, I believe that we already have some knowledge about what may work and what generally does not work well. Better enforcement of human rights standards, public health and protection plans that emphasize prevention and early intervention, and initiatives to minimize the chances and the seriousness of offending and re-offending are promising approaches.

In particular, we must repeat as a mantra that prevention is possible. Easy access to small arms and the recurrent and banal use of institutionalization are clear warning signs. Well-structured and easily accessible cultural and leisure facilities for youth, as well as improved integration of public schools with their communities, are essential. One evident problem that every government must face is the fact that appropriate measures will require time to have a durable impact.

They also will require sustained institutional reforms. In this respect, it is possible that the fragmented and frequently quite superficial preventive responses already in place in the region may produce even more adverse effects. Even in El Salvador, after the Mano Dura, the country tried to complement the plan with the so-called Mano Extendida (extended hand), a formal effort to provide assistance to former gang members who want to be rehabilitated. So far, unfortunately, this has been just a gesture of good intentions.

Since the promulgation of the preventive mantra, many fragmented programs have been developed in Latin America, sponsored by national and international, governmental and non-governmental organizations. It is of course vitally important to mobilize and empower communities and to promote human rights education. Yet, if these initiatives are not accompanied by consistent improvements in the state apparatus, if there is not a radical change in the functioning of the public security and judicial systems, then these efforts will not be successful, and they may even increase frustration and skepticism with regard to democratic institutions.

For the benefit of young people and the societies in which they live, it is imperative that Latin America's criminal justice systems be rendered not only more efficient but also more credible and accountable. Additionally, these systems need to be more accessible to the marginalized population that requires them the most—a population, including youth, that is normally distant from and fearful of the state's security and justice apparatus.

It is also crucial to develop a more reliable data bank on security issues. The absence of good information on youth violence and the efficacy of responses to it renders effective policy making more difficult and any form of evaluation impossible. And it is important to consider disproportionate media attention to youth violence as part of the information problem.

Above all, it is essential to ensure that all measures taken are viewed not only as matters of security, but also as human rights issues. Even if we are speaking about specific preventive measures, we are dealing with basic rights that have to be respected for the full development of human beings. In this respect, for example, the proper functioning of the education system is essential not only because it reduces the vulnerability of children to violence, but also because it serves a fundamental right of every child.

The Rights of Youth

Today, more than ever, it is clear that democracy and human rights are inseparable. Thus, we must assess the protection of human rights in tandem with the development of democracy. Publics across Latin America, pandered to by politicians, are calling for and accepting increasingly repressive measures in an effort to stem youth violence. But democracy demands the participation of children and adolescents and their recognition as full citizens (not as mini-human beings with minihuman rights). This means they have the right to be informed, to express opinions, and to be heard. It also means that economic, social, and cultural rights for youth are critical because, without access to health and education and a secure livelihood, young people cannot enjoy their civil and political rights in the future.

Democracy and the protection of human rights, including the rights of youth, are both works in progress, mutually reinforcing, and fragile. Born in the early stages of Latin America's democratization, repressive measures that have targeted youth gangs and criminalized the younger generation threaten the progress of both human rights and democracy. Leaders and citizens in the region must exercise their best efforts to ensure they are dismantled.

Paulo Sérgio Pinheiro *is a United Nations Independent Expert who led preparation of the 2006* UN Secretary General's Study on Violence Against Children. *He is a research associate at the University of São Paulo's Center for the Study of Violence, which he founded in 1987, and a commissioner with the Inter-American Commission on Human Rights. He was assisted in the preparation of this essay by Marcelo Daher, a project specialist with the office of the High Commissioner for Human Rights in Geneva.*